Church Without Walls

to Barbara

with very best wishes,

Graham Tomlin

Church Without Walls

A global examination of cell church

Edited by Michael Green

PATERNOSTER PRESS

Paternoster Press is an imprint of Authentic Media,
P.O. Box 300, Carlisle, Cumbria, CA3 0QS, UK
and
P.O. Box 1047, Waynesboro, GA 30830-2047, USA
Website: www.paternoster-publishing.com

British Library Cataloguing in Publication Data
A catalogue record for this book is available from the British Library.

ISBN 1-84227-139-3

Cover Design by FourNineZero
Typeset by WestKey Ltd, Falmouth, Cornwall
Printed in Great Britain by Cox and Wyman, Reading, Berkshire

Contents

Contributors

Moses Tay was the seventh Bishop of Singapore (1982–2000) with jurisdiction over Singapore, Indonesia, Thailand, Laos, Cambodia and Vietnam. He retired in 2000, after his term as the first Archbishop of S.E. Asia.

Albert Vun is an Archdeacon and the Rector of an Anglican church on the east coast of Borneo Island. The church has over 400 cell groups and has planted ten new congregations in the last seven years. He is married with three children.

Michael Green is a lecturer at Wycliffe Hall, Oxford, and Adviser in Evangelism to the Archbishops of Canterbury and York. He has written many books and has a deep interest in evangelism and the reformation of the church.

Graham Tomlin is Vice Principal and tutor in Historical Theology and Evangelism at Wycliffe Hall, Oxford, and a member of the Theology Faculty of Oxford University. He is married with two children.

George Lings is Director of Church Army's Research Unit, 'The Sheffield Centre', publishing quarterly booklets 'Encounters on the Edge' on emerging ways of being church, including cell.

Bob Hopkins and his wife Mary are co-ordinators of the Anglican Church Planting Initiatives. They are also directors of Cluster Training and Development at St Thomas' Church, Crookes, where Bob is a curate.

Mark Francisco is currently the Senior Pastor of the Coquitlam Alliance Church in Coquitlam, British Columbia, Canada. For over twenty years, he has pastored churches known for their evangelism and small group ministry emphasis. He is married with four children.

Bill Beckham is a Cell Church Consultant and Conference Speaker. He is also President of Touch Global, a ministry supporting the Cell Church Movement, and part of Touch Family in Houston, a cell family of missionaries. He and his wife Mary are watching their family grow with grandchildren.

Chris Neal is Team Rector in Thame where 500 adults seek to express church as cell and multiple congregations. He is also Director of Evangelisation for the Oxford Diocese.

Rob Merchant is part-time curate at St John's, Harborne in Birmingham, a post he job-shares with his wife Tamsin. He is currently carrying out PhD research and completing a book on demographic change and the church. He also serves on two Evangelical Alliance advisory groups.

Introduction

Michael Green

I have been privileged to travel in many parts of the world, and to see the Christian church at work. Two things are abundantly plain.

On the one hand, traditional churches in what we used to call Christendom are all on the wane. This has been apparent at least since the Industrial Revolution, and has accelerated since the two world wars. A whole way of looking at the world, influenced by the Enlightenment has given way to what we inelegantly call postmodernism. It cannot be denied that the church in Europe and to a considerable extent in North America is in bad shape, and in Australia and New Zealand it is worse. Contemporary Western people are not, on the whole, attracted to the way we do church. Its inherited style of worship and its organisation do not appear to meet their needs. They are not impressed by hierarchical figures like clergy and pastors telling them what to do. They are not attracted by liturgical music and hymns written centuries ago. They do not want to stand up, sit down and kneel when they are told to do so: this is, after all, a customised age! They do not even want to enter the ancient churches that used to throb with large congregations throughout Europe. If they go in at all, it is as tourists.

It does not matter whether the expression of Christianity is Roman Catholic or Orthodox, Anglican or Methodist, Baptist or Reformed: the numbers attending church have been in massive decline, and in many churches no children and young people are to be seen. It would be too facile to put all this down to secularisation, which has become such a dominant force in our consumer society. The remarkable fact is that there is a spiritual quest among many people today that we have not seen for many a long decade. It may be crystals and channellers, transcendental meditation or a little mild Buddhism. It may be Stonehenge on midsummer morn or Wicca dances by moonlight. But there is an undeniable spiritual quest in the air. New Age, the new paganism and the cults have an enormous fascination for materialist, i.e. Westerners who have found that materialism does not satisfy. But it has to be said that their quest for authentic spiritual experience rarely takes them to a church. The churches have generally failed to cash in on this new spiritual trend. They remain in massive decline.

That is one undeniable fact. The other is this. Wherever you go in the Two-Thirds World you find Christians. They are multiplying faster than ever before. The statisticians tell us that somewhere between 80,000 and 100,000 people a day worldwide become followers of Jesus Christ. But the vast majority of these new members of the Christian family come from the Two-Thirds World, not the traditional Christian heartlands in Europe and America. Indeed, there are now far more non-white Christians than there are whites. This is very evident when the Pope gathers his cardinals or when the Lambeth conference, a ten-yearly gathering of the Anglican bishops worldwide, takes place. The powerful centres of Christianity as this twenty-first century develops are no longer Europe, but Latin America, sub-Saharan Africa and South-East Asia, including the massive 20,000 a day growth in China. This surprises cynics who imagine that Christianity is a white man's religion. It is vexing for those who dismiss Christianity as Western colonialism to find that the very countries that have thrown off the colonial yoke are foremost in advancing the Christian faith!

And how do these new sectors of the world church spread the gospel? It is done by friendship, by small groups, by informal meetings in homes. You do not need a church building or a clergyman in order to grow the church. You do need men and women who are passionate for Jesus Christ and determined to make him known. And it seems that in the Two-Thirds World they have lots of Christians like that. I know a number of their leaders, and they seem to be ablaze and fearless for Jesus Christ. In comparison with them, I feel ashamed at the coldness and formalism of our Christianity in the West, our bondage to tradition, our captivity to buildings, and our lack of prayer, witness and confidence in the gospel, which seems to afflict so much of the Western church.

Can we humble ourselves and learn from our brothers and sisters in less developed lands? To be sure, we cannot go directly from their situation to our own. But we can, perhaps, learn some invaluable principles to try here in the West. The one most effective in Asia and Latin America is the cell church. And that is what this book is about.

There is nothing faddish about the cell church. It is not the latest bandwagon to climb on to. It is nothing less than original Christianity. It was one of the most effective expressions of the New Testament church. Romans 16 shows that this is how the church was organised in the first century. We search in vain for a papacy, but there were house churches all over the place. Somehow, however, over the centuries we have managed to lose the small, accountable group, committed to serve one another and win new Christians. In the countries I have mentioned above they find cell one of the fastest means of growth and one of the best ways of caring for church members. For the cell is the primary form of caregiving. It makes for close friendships. It enables needs to be known, prayed for, and met. It throws up lay leaders who have the gifting and the training to care for a small group. It is not dependent on ecclesiastical buildings – a home is ideal and is, moreover, non-threatening for newcomers.

John Drane, Robert Warren and others in England, along with Leith Anderson and Bill Hybels in America are exploring new forms of church. They are looking for congregations committed to mission and not merely to maintenance. But unquestionably one of the most effective forms worldwide for church growth, nurture and evange-lism is the cell church.

Little has been written about the cell church in the UK. The talented Anglican clergyman Phil Potter has recently produced an attractive book *The Challenge of the Cell Church* (Bible Reading Fellowship, 2001) and has been touring the country for the Church Pastoral Aid Society, opening people's eyes to the possibilities of the cell church, whose value he has proved over more than a decade. But most Christians know little about it. They think that a cell is just another name for a home Bible study (if they think about it at all). Their home Bible studies are probably stale, and they do not imagine that cells have anything to teach them.

If you feel like that, read this book. It will open your eyes to the vast spread of cell churches in different parts of the world, and the hope they offer for providing one of the best ways of being church in a world where religion is a leisure option, and the gospel needs to be presented in a way that attracts people's attention and meets their needs. And in an age when many have no desire to belong to an institution, but are deeply committed to a small circle of friends, the cell has a great deal to offer. It is my conviction that in the next 50 years the West will discover cells as a powerful tool for evangelism, nurture and leadership training. This, under God, may well mean a renewal of the Christian faith in the West. That is my prayer, and that is why I believe this book is an important contribution, bringing stories of the value of cell from many parts of the world.

All but two of the authors in this book are Anglicans, and this is quite intentional, for most of the existing literature on the subject comes from distinguished non-Anglicans such as Lawrence Khong and Ralph Neighbour. It could be thought that in so historic and traditional a church as the Anglican, cell churches would be inappropriate or even impossible. This book shows that this is far from being the case. Moreover, all but three of the authors in this book are not professional writers on interesting ecclesiastical possibilities. They are practitioners. They have done it. They have seen its fruitfulness. It would be wise to listen to them as they recount something of the cost and the joy of moving into cells.

Michael Green

Wycliffe Hall,
Oxford University,
Christmas 2001

1

Cell Church in Singapore

Moses Tay

Who Cares?

'We seem to have so many friends we want to greet at Christmas,' I said to my wife as I struggled to send out our Christmas letters and cards on time. 'But how many of them can be our "midnight friends" in times of personal or family crisis?' she replied. It was a sobering moment, and we were hard put to answer the question. Both my wife and I were working in demanding circumstances, and we had schoolgoing children in a competitive Singapore environment. I was then the director of a general hospital and also the priest in charge of a newly planted church in the north of Singapore.

Our quest for intimate friends and a caring community happily found the answer in our cell group. It grew up naturally in the context of the new and growing church. We were not satisfied with meeting only on Sundays for the usual service and on Thursdays for the exciting prayer and praise evening. Members of the cell group met one another's social needs, as well as other needs, during the week. For example, when a member was ill, another would take his children to school. Non-Christian friends were brought to our home cell meetings as well as to our church. We grew happily as a caring community.

However, my happiness in that caring community did not last long, because of an unexpected change of job.

No eye has seen,
   no ear has heard,
no mind has conceived
   what God has prepared for those who love him. (1 Cor. 2:9)

This had been the Lord's personal word to me, and it has become like a kaleidoscope bringing an exciting vision at every turn.

Twenty Years Ago

When I unexpectedly became Bishop of Singapore in 1982, the wind of charismatic renewal had been blowing fairly strongly for a decade. Renewed lay people were beginning to want to play a role in pastoral and spiritual ministry. However, the existing pattern was 'one man one parish', as the Anglican Church was clergy-centred. There were no non-ordained pastoral workers and the main activity of our churches was the Sunday Service. There were hardly any cell groups apart from the handful of Bible study groups for the more enthusiastic members of our cathedral.

The pastoral system had worked reasonably well, provided the clergy-shepherd knew the sheep and cared for them personally. However, this subtly reinforced an attitude of church maintenance rather than mission. But as the churches grew, the one-man-one parish system soon proved inadequate. Even a hard-working clergyman could not give adequate personal attention to more than 100–200 members. With the growth of the church, the clergy were fast becoming the bottleneck, and sometimes the cork of the bottle.

In multicultural and multilingual Singapore the move of the Holy Spirit in the 1970s and 1980s had brought in many unchurched people who were far from being monochrome. Services in different languages or dialects became necessary. The young people from different youth cultures and subcultures were not attracted to the traditional services, to put it mildly. The need for new forms and variety in church services became more acute as many of the new Christians brought their parents to church. The role of the clergy changed quickly and dramatically. No longer could the clergy remain the only pastors and teachers. The growing expectations and demands on them made ministry in the traditional mould impossible. An alternative system for pastoral care and evangelism had to be found. The new wine of the Holy Spirit in renewal and mission was clamouring for a new wineskin.

An Inspiration

The Full Gospel Church at Yoido in Seoul, Korea, burst into the limelight as the largest church in the world, growing rapidly under the dynamic leadership of Dr Yonggi Cho. In May 1985 I visited his church with my predecessor Bishop B.I. Chiu and other leaders to see for ourselves what was happening. We were impressed and inspired by what God was doing at the crowded Sunday services, the famous Prayer Mountain, their vision for church growth, evangelism and missions, and in particular, their cell groups.

The cell system stood out as the new wineskin for the new wine of the Holy Spirit. It secured the evangelistic thrust of the church and satisfied the pastoral need of its members, then moving towards the half-million mark. The cells also provided the framework for intensive prayer, dynamic witness, and ministry of lay people in the context of optimal community life – the home.

We took back above all else the model of the cell church. Would it work for Singapore? Could it be adapted into the Anglican structure of a growing diocese? Dr Yonggi Cho's book *Successful Home Cell Groups* was recommended for our clergy and lay leaders to study.[1] Learning from Korea, many of our churches started Home Cell Groups (also called by various other names) with a variety of functions, such as Bible study, prayer, fellowship, evangelism, social support and community life.

A Diocesan Attempt

In 1988 our synod asked for a training conference on this important subject. In response the diocese prepared as a priority four weekly sessions of intensive teaching and interaction on cell group ministry for leaders. Each session was taught twice in the same week to make sure that all clergy and lay leaders were able to attend. They were held in January and February 1990 in two of our largest parishes, St Andrew's Cathedral and the Church of Our Saviour. The instructors included the bishop and the leading clergy in the cell group ministry. Over 500 cell group leaders completed the teaching conference and

1 Paul Yonggi Cho, *Successful Home Cell Groups* (Logos International, 1981).

they gave fresh impetus to the growth of cell groups in the diocese and its parishes.

The four sessions at this conference covered the following topics:

1. A vision of home cell groups.
2. A basic understanding of small-group dynamics in cell group ministry.
3. Cell group and church growth.
4. Leadership in the cell group.

These sessions were designed to meet the acknowledged needs of the local church and to address deficiencies in the Anglican system as operated in Singapore.

The weakest link in the discipleship chain was often that between cell group leader and members. Usually this was because the cell leaders saw their groups as Bible study or fellowship cells. The tendency was to concentrate on the 'maintenance' function, and the cell groups failed to fulfil their evangelistic and disciple-making potential.

As cells were viewed as 'primary' groups,[2] pastors had naturally been keen to multiply their number. This had sometimes resulted in a lowering of qualifications and quality of the cell group leader, which in turn led to a decrease in effectiveness and even the lifespan of the cell group.

An underlying concept in the development of these cells was that Jesus' ministry of preaching, teaching, healing and deliverance could occur, by his grace and sovereign will, in the cell groups. Functioning as mini-congregations did not mean that the cell had to do the same thing as the church service on Sundays! However, the vital ministries of worship, teaching of the word, discipling, evangelism, counselling and ministering to

---

2 Eddie Gibbs, *I Believe in Church Growth* (Hodder & Stoughton, 1981).

one another were carried out in the cell group in deep
and personal ways. Some cell groups even organised
overseas short-term missions.

The need to cater to non-Christians (now commonly
called 'pre-believers'), new believers, and children of
members had long been recognised. Many and varied
attempts were made to address these needs. For example,
some larger home cell groups functioned in subgroups of
smaller cells according to sex, maturity level, or the stage
of life (e.g. teenagers, married couples, or the elderly). But
many preferred a mixed group as this was natural for
a family setting and evoked an enriching variety of experience and perspective from the members. Some cells
adopted a multilevel approach, such as evangelistic cells
(for pre-believers), discipling cells (for new believers) and
leadership cells (for grooming new leaders). Others
adopted the system of 'open' cells (for all, often with an
evangelistic thrust), and 'closed' cells (for specific groups
of believers). In all these attempts we were neither totally
successful nor fully satisfied.

It is obvious that with whatever cell system or emphasis
the church adopted, the cell group leader is the key to the
life of the group. As a diocese, we agreed that cell group
leaders should meet the New Testament qualifications for
elders and deacons as in 1 Timothy 3 and Titus 1:5–9. Each
parish would develop its own system for selection and
training of the cell group leaders, as well as for the opera-
tion and supervision of cell groups in the parish. Some of
the parishes followed through the development of cell
groups with a regular group leaders' retreat or special
training as the parish cell system continued to be modified.

However, while most of our churches had benefited
from cell groups that allowed the ministry of lay people,
these cell groups did not prove to be the new wineskin for
the new wine of the Holy Spirit in our churches. All too

often the clergy and the parishes continued to do what seemed right in their own eyes!

The New Cell Church Movement

While Dr Yonggi Cho, senior pastor of Yoido Full Gospel Church of Seoul, Korea, successfully pioneered the first generation of cell churches, a new cell church movement was fast emerging in Singapore. In 1990 Dr Ralph W. Neighbour Jr came to Singapore and teamed up with Lawrence Khong, a Baptist pastor who started the new Faith Community Baptist Church (FCBC) in 1986. Lawrence Khong basically put legs to Ralph's ideas on the cell church. Together they translated the cell church concepts into reality in the context of a local church. The cell church movement did not merely bring in another set of programmes, but became *the new wineskin* for the church as the new wine of the Holy Spirit was being poured out afresh across the world. Today, FCBC is more than 10,000 strong, and is moving on intensively in strategic intercession and serving the community without strings attached, in order to bring in the harvest. Lawrence Khong tells the story of FCBC in his book *The Apostolic Cell Church*,[3] which offers practical strategies for growth and outreach.

It is not easy to get a proper perspective of history when we are caught up in the excitement of the new things God is doing in our day. However, some strategists[4] give us the perspective that while Martin Luther was instrumental in a *reformation of theology*, and the Moravians in a *reformation*

---

3 Lawrence Khong, *The Apostolic Cell Church* (Touch Ministries International, 2000).
4 Wolfgang Simson, *The DAWN Report* (DAWN Ministries, 1999).

of spirituality, God is now touching the wineskins themselves, initiating a Third Reformation, a *reformation of structure*. The new wine of the Holy Spirit in our day calls out
for new wineskins (Luke 5:37, 38). And yet the cell church
actually goes back to New Testament times!

Basically, in the philosophy of cell church, the cell *is* the
church, which is radically different from a church with
cells. The cell ministry is not a department of the church,
but the various departments of the church are there to
serve the cells to which every member must belong.
The cells, in turn, provide the structure through which
members may become involved in various church
programmes.

Every cell is expected to grow in size by evangelism,
and to divide within 12 to 18 months. If a cell fails to multiply or plant another cell, it is deemed unhealthy. It may be
closed and members placed in other cells that are spiritually vibrant. Evangelism is the priority.

The cells are well structured for close supervision. In
Singapore three or four cells cluster to form a subzone
supervised and pastored by a volunteer zone supervisor.
Up to ten subzones network to create a zone of 300 to 600
people pastored by a full-time zone pastor. Five or more
zones form a district, under an experienced district pastor
who cares for 1,500 people or more. This cell church
structure enables tight supervision and effective leadership training, resulting in massive mobilisation of the
members.

Cells are linked together geographically in congregations that provide a wider network of relationships. These
congregations spell out the vision of the church in more
concrete terms, and communicate them to every cell and
every member. At the same time, each congregation can
develop its own vision within the overall vision of the
church, and manage its own programmes.

The weekly cell meetings are also structured to follow a standard four-segment agenda of *welcome, worship, works* and *word*. The cell meeting begins with a warm *welcome* of newcomers, and introduction of the members. The members then participate in an 'ice-breaker', a light-hearted activity that facilitates relationship in the group. The most powerful part is the *worship* when, for at least half an hour, members focus on delighting in the Lord. As the presence of the Lord is manifested and experienced, members minister to one another with the gifts of the Holy Spirit, and healing and deliverance may take place. The meeting then enters into the *works* stage when members pray for unsaved friends and for upcoming evangelistic events. At the *word* stage, members focus on the word of God and his dealings in their lives. In some churches the cells discuss the text and sermon of the previous week. While the cell meeting agenda is fairly standard, there can be creative variations in each of the four segments.

In the cell church structure, learning takes place through experiences in the cells. Leaders are chosen and equipped through the cells, and every member must be mobilised through the cells. The clear focus is evangelism of the community by the cell through the gifts of the Holy Spirit. Most of the fast-growing churches in Singapore are cell churches with evangelism as the priority. At the same time, all the functions of the church are integrated within the cells.

While cell church structure is an important key for growth, the structure itself does not guarantee growth. The indispensable ingredients for growth include the power of the Holy Spirit, a clear vision for and commitment to win people for Christ, and a strong leadership. Strong leadership, often caricatured as superstars, is more than a matter of style and personality. It is a godly *team* appointed and anointed by the Lord, and yet allowing the man of God to lead.

The Transition to Cell Church

The transition from a 'traditional' church structure to the cell church structure is difficult but not impossible. Archdeacon Albert Vun's experience in Chapter 7 of this volume is instructive. The prerequisites for transition to the cell church include commitment to a clear vision and strategy for growth, reliance on the supernatural work of the Holy Spirit, and strong anointed leadership. Without these, the last state of the church may be worse than the first!

Transition to the cell church does not happen naturally. It must be a clear leadership decision. As a start, it would be helpful for the pastor to set out to lead a cell group himself. The leadership of the church must be convinced to want the change. Cell group leaders need to be trained systematically. The cell structure and the new operating system need to be understood before implementation. Traditional mindsets, habits and structures will have to give way. Resistance to change will need to be overcome. Happily there is a wealth of resources in Singapore on which churches can draw if they want to make the transition – it is not necessary to reinvent the wheel or to repeat common mistakes in the transition.

Pastor Lawrence Khong, mentioned above, has conducted cell church conferences in Singapore and in other countries for the benefit of the wider church of whatever denomination. His church and the related *TOUCH Resources Pte Ltd* have been helpful resources. Through him and others, cell churches have been established in Taiwan, India, Japan, the Philippines and other Asian countries. Willie Crew of World Mission Center, Pretoria, South Africa, has appreciated Lawrence Khong's willingness to share his heart with thousands of leaders in Africa, and this is bearing much fruit today. The Bread of Life Church in Taiwan has recently grown from 3,000 to 6,000. The cell church has flourished both in cities and rural areas. For example, in the Philippines, cell churches have flourished in many villages, and have grown and spread literally from one mountain to another.

Special mention must be made of the Trinity Christian Centre, one of the leading churches in Singapore, for its willingness to help churches and leaders from around the world. Senior Pastor Naomi Dowdy and her team of anointed pastors have given strong leadership in missions, in training, and in cell church development to countries outside Singapore. Some of the pastors, like Dominic Yeo, are prepared to help churches to make the transition to the cell church. They then undertake to continue to help for a further two years. This is a valuable 'after-sales' service to ensure successful transition.

Personal Perspective

When this new generation of cell churches began, some of the initial dogmatic and exclusive statements or claims were unhelpful. Thus the insistence by some cell church proponents that everything had to be done in the cell was unfortunate. The structure of the human body with organs and cells is instructive. If we concede that there is a need for specialised cells, then it is best for these to be grouped together to function as an organ of the body. Some functions cannot be done by a single cell but rather by a group of cells, equivalent to an organ. For example, it would take a group of cells, specialised if need be, to fulfil a specific function such as music ministry in a congregation, or a community service project.

Most of the growing independent charismatic churches in Singapore are cell churches, but their cell systems are not identical. This is because of differences in philosophy and varying emphases on evangelism, fellowship and Bible study. Leadership development is even more varied in the different cell churches, and is best achieved in house and tailored to meet the vision and mission emphases of the particular church. This must inevitably raise questions about the relationship between cell church leadership training and the theological seminaries.

The leadership development in the cell church would seem to favour those with the gift of evangelism. The leaders of the more rapidly growing and dividing cells are likely to be the ones to rise in the leadership of the cell church system. But the leaders identified and trained in the cell churches may be very different from those from the traditional systems. After many years of observation and personal involvement in leadership training, however, I am convinced that leaders identified and trained through the cell churches are not inferior to those trained in the traditional systems.

The authority structure of the cell church may be quite different from that in a particular denomination. In particular, the authority of the bishop in the Anglican Church may need to be redefined, and the system of licensing workers may need to be modified. But bishops need not become an endangered species, unless they cease to walk closely and humbly with the Lord.

The distinctive strengths of the cell church include dynamic evangelism, an effective system of pastoral care, equipped lay people, sound community life, and a mobilised church, which results in dynamic church growth and is well poised for missions. There is also much room for further innovative development of the cell church system for different circumstances and for changing times. The gains in transition to the cell church far outweigh the price we have to pay. When I was in office as a bishop, I encouraged our parishes to become cell churches. My only regret is that I did not encourage them more forcefully! Although many of our parishes have appreciated the cell church, not too many have made the full transition. The Church of Our Saviour in the Diocese of Singapore has done well. So has St John's/St Margaret's Church, which has produced its own resource materials for the cell church.[5]

If we are convinced, it will take humility and courage to receive the gift of the cell church as the new wineskin for the fresh outpouring of the Holy Spirit. We shall need to be like a grain of wheat that dares to fall to the ground and die, losing our traditional identity, in order to be fruitful.

---

5 St John's/St Margaret's Church, *New Life Kit* (Armour, 1998).

2

Cell Church in Canada

Mark Francisco

One of the most dynamic ways Jesus is using to expand his kingdom in Canada is the cell church model of ministry. In my estimation those churches using the cell ministry paradigm for caring for their people and reaching the lost are becoming the flagship churches in this country. Numerous churches are reorienting and reallocating leadership responsibilities, finances and building plans to learn how to implement their ministry around small groups. The results have been greater effectiveness from both a leadership and congregational perspective.

I was first exposed to the beginnings of cell ministry some 20 years ago. In those days it was a hybrid of the popular 'Home Bible Study' ministry. That style of ministry was more teacher-to-pupil oriented and curriculum-based than the cell church model of today. It did not readily fit into a team mentality, strategic leadership development, or releasing individuals to minister according to their gifts. Today, however, through trial and error and some great practitioners who have emerged, the church is seeing God build his people and reach the lost like never before.

In this chapter I will first explain how the cell model of ministry has been effective in addressing various problems that Canadian pastors face. Secondly, I will give various examples of how small groups have been a means of transformation in the people of God. I will also summarise some of the positive characteristics of cell ministries across Canada. Finally, I will explain how, in my experience, pastors can transform their church to the small-group paradigm.

Why Has Cell Church Ministry Taken Root in Canada?

Like any new approach or technology, the cell ministry approach has been the result of pastors and church leaders grappling with problems that have plagued the church since St Paul's day. Many of the problems I faced in a small struggling church were the same that numerous other pastors faced across Canada.

One such problem has been the complexity and diversity of the needs that face people throughout the church and community. There is often a lack of the personnel and the money to meet these needs. As a child I grew up in a rural church where life seemed straightforward and the needs of people were fairly simple. As a young minister, I began in an urban setting by having to deal with two child abuse cases in my first week. As a senior pastor, I quickly learned that I did not have what it took to meet the diverse needs of this congregation, let alone their complexity, which would emerge once the church grew. I realised that I could not meet all these needs, yet I knew that God wanted me to ensure that they were met. The cell church model was the answer. It allowed for the diversity of needs to be met by the various leaders and spiritual giftedness within the groups.

Another problem was this: there was far too much to be accomplished by just one pastor. I started as a lone pastor, and it was apparent that the church needed to develop leaders, hire staff, start more strategic programmes, purchase land, build new buildings, and draw people with resources to help meet the financial needs. At that time, with no one else on staff to assist me, I faced the harsh reality that there were some issues that I was not trained for. To accomplish all these things I would need to have above-average skills in a myriad of areas: for example, counselling, leadership development, pastoral care, evangelism, discipleship, long-range planning, administration, age-related programming and financial expertise. I had to prioritise activities and even people if I were to accomplish the bare essentials – but it made me feel guilty. And the burning question remained: how was this church to reach its community and fully develop its redemptive potential if I was the only one to provide all the pastoral care, leadership development, and administrative skills? The cell system motivated and allowed many people to be involved and meet the needs of all those whom God brought to the church.

Another problem that compounded the previous issues was the myth that I was the one to carry out the care ministry rather than understanding that I was to make sure that care could be accomplished through the people the Holy Spirit gifted in the church. I correctly recognised that Jesus gave the responsibility for caring for his sheep to the leaders of the local church. Error came through thinking that I was the divinely ordained person to provide all the leadership and pastoral care that were needed! I felt a heavy responsibility to do the pastoral care of the church as I was 'The Pastor' and that was what I was paid to do. One day the Holy Spirit challenged me: 'Is it your responsibility to do all the pastoral care or are you supposed to make sure that all the pastoral care is done?' Obviously the latter was my responsibility and God helped me see how to train and release others to accomplish his will.

Another problem encountered was church growth. It seems silly to cite church growth as a problem, but that is what it was! The situation was reminiscent of the experience the early church encountered in Acts 6. People care has often been the key inhibitor for churches to grow past the 200 barrier. Up to about 200 most pastors can provide personalised and professional pastoral care for each of their parishioners. But diverse and endless demands come along with a growing church, and pastoral care can be a life drain. Ephesians 4:12 instructs pastors 'to prepare God's people for works of service, so that the body of Christ may be built up'. I found that the greatest resource in the church was the people themselves. They were gifted by the Holy Spirit and called to this local body to do ministry. My responsibility was to train the people for 'works of service' by giving them hands-on training through the cell church format.

Another contributor to these problems can be the personal issues of pride, insecurity and selfishness. This was true in my own experience, and I have observed in a number of pastors across Canada that repenting of the sins of pride and insecurity has opened the floodgates for training and releasing people to do ministry. Pastors often rather enjoy being the ones to make all the decisions and spearhead anything that is accomplished. I found it fascinating that the pastors who complained that the parishioners lacked involvement were the very ones who provided no training opportunities and no avenues for developing and using the gifts of the congregation. These pastors loved to be acknowledged as great for visiting or doing recognisable ministry, but hated the flip side of the same coin, which found them responsible for the pastoral care and leadership. But the day came when I repented of this sin and publicly resigned as the main caregiver of the church. I asked the congregation to be trained and released into ministry. Only then did the whole situation turn around and God began to do amazing things.

At one point I went to visit a woman in hospital. When I checked in at the nursing station I was informed by a nurse that this lady already had too many pastors visiting her and so I was not allowed to see her. I tried to explain that I was the head pastor with congregational responsibilities, not knowing that the pastors she spoke of were our lay pastors caring for their people! She was still not impressed and I was refused entry. Later I found out that the small-group leaders (we called them lay pastors) had taken care of food and transportation for the family and were sitting with her around the clock giving more pastoral care than I ever could. In this situation, by trusting, training and releasing people for ministry, more was accomplished than if I hoarded the responsibility and tried to accomplish everything myself. Pride and arrogance keeps pastors from releasing people to do ministry. This should never be.

The prerequisite of the cell church model is that pastors must be willing to share the ministry by developing and releasing others, rather than by doing everything themselves. Many pastors are now finding the fruitfulness of this approach. I have found that this allows me more freedom to accomplish what I most enjoy and am most gifted to do.

Many pages could be written and filled with examples of how the kingdom of God has been changed and expanded as a direct result of cell-based ministry. I have seen God use small groups to introduce many people to himself and challenge a multitude of others to a deeper walk with him. Leadership has been trained, newcomers to the church have been enfolded, spiritual gifts, long hidden, have been developed and celebrated. Pastoral care is accomplished and strategic ministries are started, resourced and led by motivated people who learn to grow and serve in a community of faith rather than as individual servants. There are limitless ways that God has used small groups in reaching and developing people to become a healthy body of believers.

I know many people in small groups who, as individuals, would never be involved in an inner-city ministry to the poor; yet, as a group, they do so on a monthly basis. I recall a small group started by a mechanic who had a passion to help others, and at the same time longed to introduce mechanics to Christ. We discussed how he could participate in ministry by fixing cars and at the same time introduce fellow mechanics to Christ and develop them as leaders to further this ministry. This could be accomplished if he used a small group as the strategy. It was tremendous to watch this man catch the vision of the small group and help people in this practical way. He led a number of them to Christ, and I later assisted him in the baptismal tank as some of his mechanic friends and those he ministered to publicly declared their allegiance to Jesus.

I think of three men who were drawn together by the task of maintenance in the church building. None of them previously knew each other but through working together they later organised a small task group, two of whose members came to a living faith. I also recall numerous veteran policemen and policewomen who learned issues of trust and interpersonal skills in a small group and later bore testimony to it during their baptism.

Because the church grew so rapidly, we ran out of space for adult Christian education. So our small groups were used to educate the congregation. This delayed the high cost of a building programme and showed us that a lack of buildings should never prevent dynamic ministry. Because the congregation was in small groups, we could strategically choose a curriculum that would best challenge and encourage those particular people in their walk with Christ. Some groups studied prayer while others took on parenting. It all depended on their needs and maturity.

As the church started to grow it was difficult for me to visit and include all the new people who were starting to attend. I learned early that I could not love everyone or even know their names. The solution was to start small groups and then develop a system of placing the newcomers within existing groups.

At one point we knew of a couple whose daughter moved to the United States and was engaged to be married. Sadly, since they did not have enough money even to drive down to the wedding, the parents resigned themselves to not seeing their daughter on her special day. When this emerged at their small-group meeting, the other members secretly pulled together all the money that was needed for the trip, plus some spending money. I had the unforgettable privilege of surprising them with this wonderful gift, and later watching how this impacted many other groups to care financially for each other. It reminded me of the early church as described in Acts 2.

Other small groups have paid for a family member's tuition at college, car repair, vacations for other people, necessary medical procedures, together with computers and tools that could not be afforded. Over the years I have seen many material needs met because the small groups have been a place where normal people can be intimately known, helped and cared for. One small group showed their love to one of their members by taking time off work and helping rebuild the roof of a chicken barn that collapsed during their small-group meeting.

Because of the distance between family members and broken family relationships, many small groups have taken the place of the traditional family and replaced it with a safe place to reparent people so they can become more like Jesus. This often happened in our 12-step programme for small groups. Over the years I have seen a multitude of people receive care in such cells, regain control of their lives and develop their spiritual giftedness in order to minister to others.

Organising and managing weddings, funerals, bridal showers and other events that happen in people's lives can all be adequately delegated and accomplished with a greater personal touch within the small-group ministry. I've seen weddings for new believers organised with tremendous results within the small-group setting. One couple who were recently converted and yet still living together were challenged to sexual purity. They were honoured as their group hosted a wedding at a subsequent meeting including decorations, food and a ceremony, at which I officiated. What an impact it had on this couple, the other small-group members and the entire church when we announced what happened.

I have seen small groups take on strategic projects in the church, community, and around the world. Through working together they have deepened their love for each other and expanded God's kingdom.

Cell Ministry across Canada

My first observation is that cell ministry is not a programme. It is a new paradigm of looking at ministry with an organic rather than a programmatic mindset. With an organic mindset, concepts of birthing, people care and leadership development all emerge naturally from the group by the very nature of its participants.

The main problem with the cell ministry philosophy is that it can run in direct conflict with a programme-oriented congregation. This shows the importance of the key leaders deciding whether they are going to move towards the cell-based church or a programme-based church. Indecision on this issue will be frustrating and painful. It must be noted that a cell-based church is very different from an upgraded home Bible study programme of the past. It is a new way of how one looks at leadership development, people care, and outreach. Implementing a cell church model with a home Bible study mindset will prove to be yet another unsuccessful programme that was tried in the past, and found wanting.

Cell churches focus on leadership training. The main responsibility of the small-group leader is to train an apprentice. The strategy for doing that is to have apprentices watch and, as they are able, be involved in every aspect of people care and leading the cell. This provides a safe place for anyone to learn strategic skills while under the protective wing of an existing leader. Most people are afraid of leading a group on their own, so they never try. Apprenticeship under the cell model allows learning on the job, and most people find that by watching and learning from an existing leader they themselves can become effective small-group leaders.

Another characteristic is that these cells have created an inclusive mindset towards outside people. They are most healthy when they develop an openness for others to join. We have a careful strategy for birthing groups. But I have found that any small group that believes it cannot or will not give birth, will eventually die. It is just the same in nature: life is meant to reproduce new life.

Another characteristic of healthy small-group churches is that all key leaders including pastors, elders and staff members must agree and model this cell philosophy of ministry if they are to succeed. Some pastors maintain that cells are a great idea but they are simply too busy to be involved. This shows the congregation that the cell is not really a priority. All key leaders must agree, support and participate, so as to produce a church of small groups rather than a church with a small-group programme.

Another important characteristic for successful small groups is that the responsibility of the small-group leaders needs to be elevated to that of a lay pastor. This includes training, accountability, and public recognition on an annual basis to do this strategic ministry. To accomplish this, the senior pastor must publicly resign as *the* caregiver of the entire church and delegate the responsibility on an ongoing basis to the lay pastors. Then the preaching pastor must champion these caregivers and leaders as the most strategic ministers in the church.

Another characteristic is that these small groups are as varied as the people in them and the members of the congregation. Some will be task-oriented small groups: others will be caregiving small groups dependent on the needs, the leadership and the gifts within the group.

Monthly training and accountability are two other characteristics of healthy small-group churches. This occurs when each small-group leader is directly responsible to a leader, who has the oversight of no more than five of them. Doing this ensures that all, especially leaders, are given adequate pastoral care, accountability and encouragement.

Changing to the Small-Group Paradigm

The biggest transition lies within the mind of the pastor and the key leaders. Once they have caught this concept and support it, the remainder of the church will follow when they understand its benefits. This often starts in the mind of the leaders by dealing with control issues. The small-group ministry is based on shared leadership. It cannot happen with tight-fisted control.

Pastors must see themselves as those who develop and empower other leaders. Apart from the weekend responsibility of preaching and teaching, the pastor's responsibility is to recruit, train, release and resource other leaders. Pastors administer the global ministry while lay pastors accomplish front-line ministry. In this way, the ceremonial leadership we provide also becomes more strategic and focused.

The proof of the pudding will be in the eating: will church members follow this paradigm or not? I find that if good pastoral care is provided and spiritual growth enhanced, most parishioners will wholeheartedly embrace it. Time and again it comes back to control and care issues. Pastors must stop trying to control everything, and instead provide lay pastors with resources. Pastors must make sure that everyone is cared for, rather than either attempting to do it all themselves, or allowing everyone trying to be in control – and very few being cared for.

Conclusion

I have seen God use small groups to reach the lost, build Christians to be fully devoted followers of Christ, accomplish a variety of ministries and expand God's kingdom. Small groups have dramatically touched and changed my own life. One of the first ministry priorities of Jesus was to start a small group of 12 and through it to accomplish his ministry. He used the small-group setting to develop our church fathers. A close look at Scripture reveals that while Jesus was ministering to large groups, his strategic focus was the development of his disciples (Matt. 5:1b–2). Jesus' ministry emphasis was directed towards a small group of disciples and through them he would change the world. We would do well to follow his example.

3

The Church with Two Wings

Bill Beckham

A different kind of church burst upon the world scene shortly after World War II. Independent of each other, several creative churches began to use small groups as an organising principle of ministry. These early models attracted attention and challenged other leaders to add small groups to their churches. Consequently, for the past 40 years a significant number of churches across the world have experimented with small groups, with varying degrees of success.

This widespread interest in small groups has several different streams and names but is often called 'the Cell Church Movement'. In this chapter I explain why I also use the term 'the two-winged church'. Shakespeare reminds us that 'a rose by any other name would smell as sweet'. What the church is called is not as important as how the church operates and what it accomplishes.

Visions, Dreams and Failed Programmes

Some churches have successfully established small groups as a viable ministry option, while other sincere leaders and good churches have repeatedly failed. Normally a church is unwilling to give a second chance to a failed programme. But, during a period of several decades, many of the same church leaders have tried to make groups work four and five different times using the latest small-group method. Why this attraction to groups despite the difficulty and failure? I believe God is at work in this unaccountable fascination with small groups and the abnormal tolerance for failure when trying to use them.

Through the prophet Joel and the apostle Peter God promised that the pouring out of the Spirit would result in young men having visions and old men dreaming dreams (Joel 2:28–32; Acts 2:17–21). Since the time of Christ, God's visions and dreams of the church to young and old alike have included small-group community. Through his revelatory visions and recurring dreams God seems to be saying to leaders today, 'Small-group community is important to me, and you will do it until you get it right.' In the first decade of the twenty-first century many churches are beginning to 'get it right' about small-group community.

A Parable of the Church

I have tried to make small groups work in the church during 40 years of ministry. More than a decade ago a little story dramatically changed how I perceive the church. The parable of the two-winged church came to me as a personal epiphany one Saturday afternoon after a stimulating but frustrating discussion about the church with a group of university students. This simple story is now the paradigm, point of reference, and organising principle that fits the different pieces and parts of the church together for me.

Once upon a time God created a church with two wings. One was a large-group wing and the other a small-group wing. With these two wings the church could soar high into the heavens, come into the presence of the Creator and do his bidding over all the earth.

One day the wicked serpent, who had no wings, came to the two-winged church and said, 'Do you know you can fly with just one wing? Yes! You can fly with just a large-group wing.' And so the church that had been created with two wings began to try to fly with just the large-group wing. And sure enough, if it beat that large-group wing long enough and hard enough it could get airborne. But it never flew very high, never went very far from its original take-off point; and, as one-winged things are prone to do, often it went round in circles. But it could fly.

And so from that time in the fourth century the church that had been created as a two-winged church used only the large-group wing. Finally the small-group wing atrophied at the side of the two-winged church.

From time to time the church remembered those days in the past when it had soared high into the heavens, and had come into the presence of the Creator to do his bidding over all the earth. But now it was too late. The two-winged church had become a one-winged, earthbound institution.

So, one day the Creator returned and recreated another two-winged church: with a large-group wing and a small-group wing. Once again the church could soar high into the heavens, come into the presence of the Creator and do his bidding over all the earth.

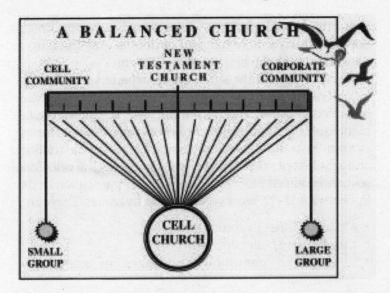

The kernel truth in this parable is that the church is balanced between corporate community and cell community: between a large-group expression and a small-group expression.

The Nature of Cell Community

According to historian Herbert Butterfield:

> The strongest organizational unit in the world's history would appear to be that which we call a cell because it
> - is a remorseless self-multiplier
> - is exceptionally difficult to destroy
> - can preserve its intensity of local life while vast organizations quickly wither when they are weakened at the centre
> - can defy the power of governments
> - is the appropriate lever for prising open any status quo.

Butterfield concludes that cells seem to be 'the appointed way by which a mere handful of people may open up a new chapter in the history of civilization'.[1]

Christ designed the small-group experience so that his followers in every age can live in his incarnation presence, resurrection power and eternal purpose. In its New Testament form the small group or cell is as warm and nurturing as a family, as disciplined and focused as a squad of soldiers and as self-contained and cohesive as a biological cell. Consequently, in cell life every member can participate in the Ephesians 4:11–12 'works of service' in five areas. They can

- abide in Christ in community;
- care for new believers;
- live out the 'one another passages' in accountable relationships;
- develop necessary nurturing leaders;
- reach out in evangelism and ministry.

The modern expression of the cell has evolved over several decades into the New Testament community model through a process of trial and error. This New Testament cell unit allows the church to be a holy church and a harvest church no matter what the size of the church, its geographical location, the sociological conditions around it or the culture in which it exists.

Church Design: The Nature of God

Jesus designed the life (wine) and structure (wineskin) of the church around the most fundamental truth in the universe: the nature of God.

---

1 H. Butterfield, 'The Role of the Individual in History', in C.T. McIntire (ed.), *Writings on Christianity and History* (Oxford University Press, 1979), 24.

The *life* of the church is found in the Trinitarian nature of God. God is Father, God is Son and God is Spirit. Another way to say that God is Trinity is to say God is community. This means that the dynamic life of small-group community is rooted in the Trinitarian community nature of God. Therefore, community is the foundational truth, the first cause and the essential element in the life of the church.

The *structure* of the church reflects the 'transcendent' and 'immanent' nature of God. These two theological words are linked and mean that God's relationship to humanity is simultaneously both great (transcendent) and near (immanent). Isaiah refers to these two aspects of God's nature as 'the most high God' and 'the most nigh God' (Isaiah 57:15). God is both beyond the reach of (transcendence) and within the grasp of (immanence) humans.

C.S. Lewis explains this unique transcendent and immanent relationship in a discussion of the divine goodness of God:

> God is both further from us, and nearer to us, than any other being . . . He makes, we are made: He is original, we derivative. But at the same time, and for the same reason, the intimacy between God and even the meanest creature is closer than any that creatures can attain with one another.[2]

Every Christian *personally* experiences God in a transcendent and immanent way through the work of the Holy Spirit. A Christian can be alone or with thousands and still experience the greatness (transcendence) and nearness (immanence) of God.

However, as a *corporate body* Christians experience the transcendent and immanent nature of God together in a special community way that we call 'church'. Within a

---

2 C.S. Lewis, *The Problem of Pain* (New York: MacMillan, 1977), 41.

large-group setting of scores, hundreds or thousands, Christians uniquely experience the greatness of God. Within a small-group setting of 3 to 12 people Christians uniquely experience the nearness of God.

Jesus built transcendence and immanence into the practical small-group and large-group design of the church in the New Testament.

The Frontal Assault on the Nature of God

During the early centuries the church was busy rebutting one theological attack after another. The Apostles' Creed, Nicene Creed and Creed of Chalcedon were some of the responses to controversies about the nature of God, Christ and the Holy Spirit. If these heresies had won the day, we would not know God personally as Father, Son and Spirit. God would be far away and unapproachable or, as in Greek mythology, God would be a man with godlike qualities or a god with manlike qualities.

Praise God, the church survived these direct assaults upon the nature of God. The early church countered Satan at every theological point until the truth about the nature of God finally triumphed and the church deservedly celebrated victory.

The Rear Assault on the Nature of God

However, while the church was busy defending the faith and winning the battles against theological frontal attacks, Satan counter-attacked from the rear. A major assault against the design of the church was launched in the fourth century during the time of the Roman emperor Constantine.

Satan attacked the small group: the place where the nature of God could be experienced and lived out in practical, everyday community. Consequently, small-group community and spiritual ministry by ordinary Christians were virtually eliminated. The church was restructured as an institution dependent on a building and professional leaders. For good measure, the church was married to the state and became either the lord or the servant of political powers and institutional religion.

Through this rear assault on the design of the church Satan was able to accomplish what he could not do from the direct frontal attacks on the nature of God. Even though the church won the victory at the point of theology, it had already lost a major battle at the point of the application of that theology in practical New Testament community.

As a testimony to his grace and power, God has used the Constantinian model in spite of the collateral damage it caused to the life and power of the church. I stand in awe of what God has accomplished through the one-winged church. At the beginning of the twenty-first century the church is positioned for a worldwide harvest. The way God has used and blessed the one-winged church gives me hope for the future of the two-winged church. If God has been able to do what he has done through Constantine's one-winged church, what *can* he do through the New Testament two-winged church?

Parallel Streams in History

A strong case can be made that God has continued to work through a parallel large-group/small-group stream that flowed throughout history alongside the traditional model established by Constantine. For several reasons, the specifics about this kind of church in history are not well documented.

First, books were rare and books about alternate ways of being church were not high on the ecclesiastical or political publishing list. Second, the people writing and editing the books were killing the people doing church differently. 'Heretics' don't get much good press. Third, these streams had to exist beneath the radar screen of those in power. Out of sight, out of mind was a principle of survival. Fourth, like Jesus with the authorities of his day, these movements were considered insignificant and unimportant compared with the 'real' events of history.

Finally, modern historians, preoccupied with the traditional paradigm of church have overlooked a different model. Connecting the dots of community from the first century to modern times is difficult enough when one is looking for community. But, when Constantine's cathedral rather than Christ's community is the working paradigm, the historical community dots are almost impossible to connect.

But they are there! Reading between the lines of what recorded history we have, one can make a good case that a more New Testament design of the church coexisted in some form with the Constantine cathedral in every century.

Patrick, Monastic Communities and Longboats

For example, as early as the fifth century in Ireland, Patrick seems to have used a more New Testament approach.[3] Irish monks and nuns were organised in monastic 'communities' that eventually became self-

---

3 See Mark Galli, *Christian History* 17, Issue 60, No. 4 (1998), 8.

supporting cities constructed like Celtic forts. It is quite probable that within their monastic life, Irish Christians experienced New Testament community.

In the sixth century the Iona community was established by the great Irish missionary Columba and is one of the best examples of this monastic community life. From that island community missionaries travelled to Scotland, England and Europe and, according to legend, even to North America. It is said that these Irish missionaries were sent out as groups of 12 in longboats to spread the gospel. Maybe that was just the size of the boat, but the number 12 and their communal living does raise the possibility that the Irish brand of Christianity had something to do with the first-century community pattern.

The Early Reformers

Most of the early reform streams had a small-group community expression in one form or another. Waldo of Lyons (Peter Valdes) founded the Waldensians, one of these early parallel movements in the twelfth century in the Piedmont region of the Alps. The motto of the Waldensians was 'Into darkness, light.' This movement operated first as a torch within the Catholic Church and eventually became a guiding light for the Reformation.

An Inquisition police report written in the fourteenth century stated that the Waldensians were divided into small groups with certain individuals responsible for the care of each group. 'These various small groups, to a certain degree, were independent, and able to pursue their particular vision of the religious life.'[4]

---

4 Giorgio Bouchard, 'An Ancient and Undying Light', *Christian History* 8, Issue 22, No. 2 (1989), 8.

Other reform streams flowed out of the theology and community structure of the Waldensians. John Hus, the great Bohemian (Czech) preacher was identified by church authorities as a Waldensian when he was martyred in 1415. Again, following the Waldensian model, the Moravians desired to return to New Testament community life and in 1457 organised a church called the Unitas Fratrum, the Unity of the Brethren, later to be known as the Moravian Church.

For several centuries these alternative streams of church life moved under the radar screen of recorded history until they burst forth as an undeniable historical reality during the Reformation.

The Reformation

An impressive monument stands in the city of Worms where Luther made his famous statement 'Here I stand. I can do no other, so help me God.' Luther is the central figure at the top of the monument but is surrounded and supported by the statues of Wycliffe, Hus, Erasmus, Zwingli and other Reformers. Many of these Reformers suffered and died not only for the theology of the church but also for the right to live out the theology of the church in a New Testament community way.

In the early days of the Reformation Luther's vision and dream of the church included small-group community. Luther considered changing the Constantinian model because he understood that reformed theology had to be lived out in a reformed structure. 'Those who want to be Christians in earnest and who profess the gospel with hand and mouth should sign their names and meet alone in a house somewhere to pray, to read, to baptize, to receive the sacrament, and to do other Christian works.'[5]

However, in the end Luther did not complete the Reformation regarding the point of structure, because of personal, practical and political reasons. Fortunately, other groups were more faithful to the structural implications of Reformation theology.

Zinzendorf and Wesley

In 1722 Count Zinzendorf began to assemble Bohemian and Moravian Brethren and Pietists on his German Saxony estate in a special community called Herrnhut. This Moravian community eventually spread the gospel to five continents and influenced the Methodist revival and Baptist mission movement.

John Wesley was deeply moved by the New Testament life of these groups. Wesley visited Herrnhut in 1738 and later adopted many of its features and terminology. His journal reveals his impressions of that community during his brief stay. 'I would gladly have spent my life here … Oh, when shall this Christianity cover the earth as the waters cover the sea?'[6] Eventually God answered that question through Wesley's own large- and small-group movement, which covered England 'as the waters cover the sea'.

The Cell Church Movement emerging in the twenty-first century is built upon the theological and practical legacy of first-century Christianity that was lived out at great sacrifice in these other periods of history.

---

5 'Preface to the German Mass and Order of Service', in Paul Zeller Strodach (trans.), *Luther's Works* (Fortress, 1965), 53:63–4.
6 *The Works of John Wesley* (3rd edn.; 1872) 142;Vol. 1 'Journals', Oct. 14, 1735 to Nov. 29, 1745; Sat. Aug. 12, 1738.

Conclusion

At a recent conference in Sydney, Australia, a book prize was given to the three or four churches that wrote the best explanation about 'What the Cell Church means to me'. Some of the answers were quite moving and lengthy. I still remember the answer from one church that caused the greatest stir among the leaders at the conference. The submitted paper had one word on it: 'HOPE!'

I was surprised by the use of only one word. But I was not surprised by the word that was used. I have found that 'hope' is a word often associated with the Cell Church Movement.

I believe New Testament community gave hope to Patrick and Columba in the midst of pagan Ireland. Peter Valdo of the Waldensians must have had great hope and encouragement because of the small groups that God used in his day to restore New Testament life. And, I believe, martyrs such as Hus died with great hope not only because of the promise of heaven but because of the New Testament small-group communities they left behind.

His small groups also gave hope to John Wesley. Upon discovering his 'classes' or small groups he declared, 'At length, while we were thinking of quite another thing, we struck upon a method for which we have cause to bless God ever since.' After hearing the reports from the first small-group meetings Wesley added, 'This is the thing; the very thing we have wanted so long.'[7]

God has also placed this word into my heart. After serving three traditional churches as pastor, 15 years as a missionary and more than a decade of researching and

---

7 Michael Henderson, *John Wesley's Class Meetings* (Nappanee, IN: Evangel Publishing House, 1997), 80.

living in a cell church, I have hope. I have hope that the church can

- mobilise every member for ministry;
- be a holy church in an unholy world;
- harvest the billions to be born in the next decades;
- assimilate new believers and nurture them to maturity;
- be a dynamic witness in every political, social, economic and religious situation;
- fulfil the great longing of Christ that his earthly body live in unity;
- take the Good News into Jerusalem, Judea, Samaria and the world;
- be the 'pure and blameless' bride of Christ;
- be one against which 'the gates of hell will not prevail'.

This hope is misplaced if it is in some new small-group structure or method. However, if my hope is in the nature of God as Father, Son and Spirit and the nature of God as transcendent and immanent, my hope is assured because it is built on nothing less than God himself.

4

Cell Church: A New Way of Being?

Bob Hopkins

Many have described cell church as a whole new way of being church.[1] 'At last, I've found what I signed up for,' says Anglican vicar Kerry Thorpe, who leads a cell church in Kent. And it is a new way of *being*, rather than *doing*, because folk speak of the sense of having discovered a new depth of relationships and quality of community. More profoundly still, it may be a new way of *seeing* church.

Bill Beckham has helpfully shown in the previous chapter that at the birth of 'Christendom', under Constantine, the church went through a critical change and, in its institutional form, began to focus exclusively on its large group or 'wing'. While I was inspired by Beckham's thesis, I was left wondering how such a defective one-winged church survived the following 16 centuries. Praise God for his grace!

---

1 See, e.g., Ian Freestone, *A New Way of Being Church* (Sold Out, 1995). The booklet is now printed and distributed by Anglican Church Planting Initiatives, Crookes Endowed Centre, Crookes, Sheffield, S10 1UB (www.acpi.org.uk).

However, it dawned on me that the life of the church survived precisely because the small-group functions of community and discipleship *did* continue. I analyse the shift after Constantine somewhat differently from Bill Beckham. As the Christian faith permeated Roman society the mission function of the church shifted from making disciples of the pagan majority to discipling the next generation, to sustain Christendom. This function was gradually transferred from the minority sectlike cells in a hostile environment, to the basic building block of society – the extended family, into which believers were incorporated. This is exactly consistent with previous biblical revelation. There was a strong Jewish tradition of the extended family expressing all aspects of the life of the people of God. Worship and learning the faith story were central to the daily, weekly and annual rhythms of family life. Traditions and rituals such as the shared cup, Sabbath readings and yearly celebrations nurtured and sustained them.

The Christian extended family (*oikos*), which followed this trend, remained the crucial aspect of mission in forming and conforming the next generation to the vision and values of the covenant people of God. Here they learnt the Scriptures (with visual aids on clothing and doorposts). The extended family was also where worship became a natural way of life in the regular Sabbath meal and Passover celebration. Here is also where they discovered how to apply these biblical principles to establish godly habits and a disciplined lifestyle. This has been the 'small wing' of the church (see previous chapter), and the new way of seeing it is to realise that when Christendom works, extended family *is* church. And down the ages, or in parts of society where this became weak, Christians established Sunday schools and small discipleship groups, to retain or regain the same small-wing function of church.

So the church still had both wings. It needed them. A church with no small-group wing at all would, in my opinion, eventually become extinct. The important difference, though, was that it had simply ceased to see or to talk of the small-group wing as 'church'.

Once we have this new way of seeing church, we realise that the present mission crisis is primarily due to the loss of the small wing of church in much of the West. But it was not lost in the third and fourth centuries so much as in the nineteenth and twentieth century, for that is when the extended Christian family dwindled away and opened the door to rapid secularisation. For this reason cell church, which is more akin to the form of the small wing in the first three centuries, now becomes increasingly vital for the re-evangelisation of the West. Beckham has rightly highlighted the appropriateness of cell-type structures in the Celtic and Wesleyan re-evangelisation of Britain. We desperately need them now.

This leads us to one further insight needed to complete my new way of seeing church and its mission on a global scale. Then I believe we can rightly see where the cell church fits. This is the recognition that we have broadly three mission contexts: Christendom, post-Christendom and the pre-Christians. Nor is it even that simple, since the vestiges of Christendom remain in some pockets in the West. So the shift to post-Christendom in today's society embodies stronger and weaker residues of the faith, and differing senses of having tried and rejected it. Moreover, there are the two distinct pre-Christian situations of culture: one where the gospel has never reached and one in those parts of Western society where it has now become unknown.

The extended family has gone, and Christian nuclear family as a place of prayer, Bible story and assimilating values is also going. Christian schools with a small-group 'discipling' element have largely disappeared. Some modern Christian nuclear families, while still keeping up family prayers, are clearly a small minority. Indeed many sociologists consider the nuclear family simply too small to provide enough stability and support to withstand today's pressures. Rocketing family breakdown statistics are one tragic consequence. Add to this the breakdown of neighbourhood and community, and we see why the door was wide open to secularisation. And this is why it is overwhelmingly important to recover the small group for mission and nurture.

But we need to learn new ways of seeing church. It is not the building; it is not a ritual on Sunday; nor is it the institution. If we free ourselves from assuming that church is defined by its *form and structure* and look instead at *function*, we might define church as 'a Jesus community of disciple-making disciples'. We are losing this function, which has for generations been most effectively performed outside and beyond the structure we called 'church'. We see the effects in struggling and dying 'churches'. We urgently need to restore the functions of discipleship and forming a Christian worldview as central to the task of the people of God. These functions, which have always been found in the small-group 'wing', are re-emerging powerfully in the cell church movement.

As a movement rather than a programme, there is a great deal of diversity in the way that cell church is developing in different contexts. Our experience has been predominantly among the European Anglican churches seeking to implement cell principles. We have come across a number of common misunderstandings, which seem to stem from a basic problem. For example, an important issue for Anglicans has been the issue of sacraments. Cell is fully church, but that does not necessarily mean that you have to do everything that is essential to church at the small-group level. Each level of church life can fulfil different roles that complement one another. Thus many cell churches keep baptisms for the Sunday gathering of all the cells, but involve a new convert's cell leader with the minister in the baptism. In the same way, Communion is ideal for Sunday celebrations, and is greatly enriched by being the time when all the cells come together to celebrate their shared lives and shared meals through the week.

The critical point to understand is that at the heart of cell church lie a group of values and principles rather than a clearly defined programme and structure. We do not believe in carbon copies! I am concerned that every few years there seems to be a wave of interest in the latest church fashion, whether it be 'seeker services', Alpha or cell church. This often seems to be driven by the consumerism of our culture or perhaps by desperation to reverse declining church attendance. The result is confused and disorientated congregations who can't keep up with the latest vision. It seems to me that all of these successful movements initially emerge because crucial principles have been prayerfully applied to a specific context. We need therefore to learn to look beyond a model or package and see the underlying principles that we can then adapt prayerfully to our own situation.

There may still be strong extended families in countries or contexts where Christendom is fading, as in Latin America and some poor estates in northern England. An important aspect of fading Christendom is that people often feel themselves culturally to be Christians. An intentional cell-based discipleship form of church may offend both their folk-religion idea of church and their pride in believing that 'We are British or Finnish, and so of course we are Christians – only sects put you through that strong discipleship stuff!' Obviously, cell insights may need a more subtle introduction here.

So armed with these perspectives, let me illustrate varied responses among churches that are seeking to move towards the cell structure, particularly from overseas. My most recent shared insights come from a sabbatical trip with colleagues in summer 2001 to Singapore, Samoa, Chile, Brazil and New Zealand.

Singapore had been a pre-Christian mission context. Therefore intentional, highly programmatic, 'pure' cell-based churches have made a breakthrough in delivering the discipleship necessary to transform the worldview of those from other religious cultures.

At the opposite extreme was Samoa where we visited for a family wedding. As well as an amazing cross-cultural challenge, this was an experience of the old days of Christendom. Christianity permeates the culture and it is sustained by the extended family (the small wing of church). A bell is rung daily at 6 p.m. in every village to announce family prayers, and visitors on incoming planes are asked to respect this with silence! On Sundays there is over 90 per cent attendance at services in church buildings, and then the extended family meets for a shared meal and discussion of common issues. One chief and head of a household explained to me, 'We often have 30 or 40: it really is church!' On leaving this family gathering all spoke individually with Granny who challenged me to live out the cross of Christ and prayed a blessing on us all. If that is not an Acts 2 church, I don't know what is. To introduce cell church in competition with this fabric of extended Christian family would be mad!

In Chile we visited a small-church plant in the northern city of Arica, which was exploring the cell concept. And in complete contrast, we worked with Alf Cooper, his elders and small-group leaders in the well-established La Trinidad Church of some 700. Whereas most of the revival growth in Chile has been among the poor, La Trinidad has unashamedly taken on the mission challenge of the elite. They are evangelising the *classe alto* – the bosses and leaders of institutions. Here a positive attitude to Catholicism is common (though few attend Roman Catholic meetings). So pure cell is much harder for the people. Another barrier was the decade of investment the church has made in programmes to equip and mobilise the whole church in ministry – itself a core cell value, but alive to a traditionalist outlook. These together had made people back off from considering cell – so highly successful in other parts of Latin America. However, as we looked at the church's stale home groups and outlined the values of cell rather than a rigid programmatic structure, the Christians there have now begun to move forward with parallel cell implementation.

In the *favelas* (shanty towns) of São Paulo where 4 million live on 'invaded land' – over sewers for example – we stayed with a Baptist project. Even a short stay on the edge of one *favela* showed us that despite drugs, violence and occult influence, the people enjoyed extended family and a level of community unknown in middle-class UK. Their birth rate is twice the city average. So the mission strategy here was to plant churches through establishing pre-schools – small discipleship groups of 8 to 12. Through the relationships made, adult small groups begin with Bible discovery and application, and learning to pray. These emerging 'small wing' expressions of church follow lines of extended family and neighbourhood. So successful have these been that 23 *favelas* in São Paulo and 19 elsewhere have church plants spearheaded by this 'small wing' church. The wife of Pele the soccer star, herself a recent convert, is so impressed, that she now sponsors the programme!

Here in the UK we see much stronger elements of the old Christendom remaining in the north of England than in the south. And much more in the poor, working-class estates. The same trends apply to the remaining expressions of extended family. Successful implementation of cell church principles needs to take these differences into account. This means that the more intentional 'pure cell' structures need to be adapted and the core principles delivered in more flexible ways.

Even more marked is the fact that the emerging generation of the under-thirties is rapidly moving back from a post-Christendom to a pre-Christian culture. Among them classic cell church is working well. Indeed it is almost the only way of reaching and holding this generation. The under-thirties are generally a mission black hole in so many UK churches. But this need not be so if cell church insights provide a place of belonging and community as well as discipleship in their discovering of Christianity – from scratch!

On the other hand, in Scandinavia formal Christendom is still strong. To be Finnish is to be Lutheran, and over 90 per cent are paid-up members of the state church. However only 2 or 3 per cent attend church. But the folk-religious consciousness holds Christian rite, symbol and the church building very high. Hence the great success of a mission project like 'Thomas Mass' in Helsinki. They began in the historic St Nicholas church building with a mixture, on the one hand, of tradition (candles, robes, sacrament) and, on the other hand, of postmodern format (tables to write spontaneous prayers; taking these prayers to baskets at the altar; participation; testimony; modern music; and so on). When we attended, the church was packed with over 1,000 seated in the pews, while others sat on the floor. However, newcomers were directed to welcome desks in the crypt for coffee and to sign up for cell-like discipleship groups. Cell principles here are creatively introduced as a follow-up phase, with the recognition that the gathering place can still be a reinvented large-wing event – celebrated on Sunday and in a church building.

Contrast this with a project in Oslo, Norway. Here a couple of Lutheran priests are creating church for the marginalised of society. They gather on a weekday in a busy city-centre street. In full view of all the passing shoppers, they don sacramental robes, set a trestle table as an altar and cover it with an embroidered cloth, and lighted candles. Then with guitars and a formal Eucharistic liturgy they draw the homeless, drug addicts, prostitutes and punks and offer them bread and wine. These are the disenfranchised who would never enter a church building: that is seen as a symbol of the oppressive power system that pushes them to the bottom. But 'Christendom' is still strong enough for bread and wine (which church legalists would refuse them) to point them to a Saviour who accepts them and gave his life for them. Here is another creative mission example of rightly seeing the remaining 'Christendom' opportunity of a radical but traditional 'large wing' gathering point. The leaders know that Christendom is only skin deep in the culture and these broken lives need structured discipleship to rebuild and instruct them. So they hire a hall next to their street corner and start 'small wing' discipleship cells for those who respond regularly. Again, consciously or unconsciously, the principle of cell, small-wing church, is being sensitively introduced, but as the supporting, not the leading, edge of mission.

Anything new presents big challenges for leaders, many of whom were trained in a system that prepared them neither to lead nor to manage change. I hope that this book will help both to stimulate them and also to assess the appropriate application and adaptation of these powerful cell principles. We found this even in the 'pre-Christian' mission context of Singapore. In our meeting with Derek Hong, the leader of the largest Anglican cell church, I asked what lessons they were learning after a decade of experience. His answer was the need for increasing flexibility in its application. Having established cell church through a strong top-down structured approach, they are now recognising the need for freeing up if they are not to lose the entrepreneurial creativity and pioneer mission spirit from the grass roots. So they are encouraging variety in types of cell and in the cells' approach to mission and outreach. The power of the principles of cell church must always be protected from the prison of legalistic programmes.

All these stories emphasise the fact that in order to adapt the principles appropriately the emphasis must be on values, not on structures. I sense that while many are put off cell by the jargon, and complex and apparently inflexible structures, others are enthralled by the theory and lose their freedom to adapt it.

The heart of cell church must be expressed in its core values. These values are not found exclusively in cell churches: they are at the very heart of the gospel. Cell church, however, in contrast to many other ways of being church, seeks to allow the values decisively to shape the way that church is structured. The success of any cell church depends crucially on these values being well communicated to and owned by as many within the church as possible. Experience shows that this ownership of values leading to a new vision must happen before structures are changed – or disaster is likely. These values are well summarised in a list adopted by the English cell church network:

- *Jesus at the centre*
  Cells are not Bible study groups, counselling groups or social groups. They are church in the home or the office. This means that it is vital that the cell meeting keeps re-

minding itself that Jesus is the focus for the meeting. He is its centre and the source of its life. He is the reason that the cell meets and the one who transforms the lives of the members. The groups are encouraged therefore to meet with the same sort of expectations as if Jesus was visibly seated in one of the armchairs.

- *Cells are communities of sacrificial love, with open and honest relationships*

  Cells are the building blocks of the church rather than an appendage to the Sunday celebration for a minority of keen members. Cells are the basic Christian community of the church. The life of the cell is measured not just by its weekly meeting but by its communal life throughout the week. For those used to home group Bible studies, it is all too easy to just change to cell jargon and structures while missing this core value. Such a group may end up with slightly more effective meetings but wondering what all the fuss about 'cell church' was about. A good cell leader works hard to model and create a sense of community so that the meeting becomes the formal gathering of that community just as the celebration becomes the gathering of all the cells that make it up. Of course, in the pressures of real life as imperfect people, any community will soon move beyond the initial honeymoon phase with all its illusions and become *dis*illusioned with one another. This is where Christian community really counts. It takes honesty and sacrificial commitment, and in the process teaches the heart of Christian love in those times when members may feel like hating or at least avoiding one another.

  The cell also includes at its fringe the friends and family of members, so that being a caring pastoral community and being effective in outreach work together rather than competing for the church's time and energy.

- *Every member ministers, using their gifts*
Cells have leaders, but the leadership style differs sharply
from the traditional home group. Leaders are not *teachers*
so much as *facilitators*. In fact it is often those who were
most naturally home group or Bible study leaders who
have the greatest difficulty adjusting to cell leadership. A
good cell leader will often say very little in a cell meeting
because he or she wants to facilitate the participation of the
members. Cell meetings normally adopt an intentional
format such as the '4 Ws' outlined below to reflect this
emphasis on everyone contributing.

- *Every member is maturing in Christ*
Open, honest relationships and application-centred content naturally create a context for accountability. This is
often instigated by cell members as an issue they discuss.
For example, the cell may be looking at the topic of forgiv-
ing others. A member who is struggling to forgive her boss
at work for seeming to show favouritism is able to receive
support and prayer from the group, but is then asked the
following week how she has been able to live it out
through the week. The cell may also be divided into prayer
partners who keep in touch through the week and are able
both to pray and keep each other accountable. As new
members join a cell, they are usually also encouraged to
work through 'equipping materials' as a systematic discipleship course with their prayer partner or 'sponsor'.

- *Everyone is involved in friendship evangelism*
It is vital to keep the vision of growth through evangelism
very high on its agenda. In Britain, where many churches
have had pastorally focused home groups for many years,
it has been all too easy for some cells to become cosy
cliques and lose the vision of reaching out, growing and
multiplying. Once again, prayer and accountability are

essential. So too is strategy. For example, a cell may spend a few weeks praying for the area in general and for their own struggles for good relationships with non-Christians. They may then focus prayer for the following few weeks on three particular 'contacts' of each cell member, at the same time encouraging lots of social events. This might then lead to an Alpha or 'just looking' course or a guest service. And so the cycle continues![2]

Cell Church follows the dictum that 'we do what we value and we value what we do'. Hence the activities of the small group are designed to ensure that the values are worked out in practice every week. Central to the weekly meeting is a structure to reflect these values. Many have adopted variations of Ralph Neighbour's 4 Ws:

1. *Welcome*
This opening to the meeting includes all sorts of activities to get to know one another better, to get everyone used to taking part in the meeting from the start, and to put any new-comers at ease. Many groups use 'Ice-breakers' or 'Quaker Questions' ensuring that no Bible knowledge or Christian jargon is used so that non-Christians and newcomers feel at ease. Beware though: these questions are often much more profound than they seem at first glance. We have found Christians who had been in home groups together for over twenty years admitting that they suddenly realised that they didn't really know one another. Many have also found that these simple questions, in eliciting snapshots of each other's stories, created understanding and compassion for those in the group they naturally found it most difficult to get on with.

---

2 Laurence Singlehurst, *Cell Church UK* 1 (autumn 1998), 3.

2. *Worship*

This is not the thin, and sometimes frankly embarrassing, imitation of congregational worship so often used in home groups. The object is to release participation and creativity as the group focuses on the fact that they meet in the presence of Christ, with Him as their focus. Singing may be useful, but there are a wealth of other ways to release a small group in praise. Many use objects, symbols, rewrite psalms in their own words, use art, poetry, or write a 'Thank You' card to God listing things he's done that week.

3. *Word*

Again it is vital to resist the temptation of imitating the teaching given in the large meeting. Cell is not the place for a mini-sermon sort of Bible study with some discussion thrown in. The key goal is less on new insight than practical application. The questions revolve more around 'how do I need to change, in order to live this?' than 'what does this mean?'

Many cells take the application of Sunday's sermon and share how it challenges them, then pray for one another. Accountability is a key ingredient, making the 'word' part of the meeting a focus to enable cell members in the costly business of counter-cultural living.

4. *Witness*

The evangelistic element of the group must be a top priority. This may include helping one another to break out of the Christian 'ghetto' and make non-Christian friends through work, sports, hobbies, social activities and community involvement. It will also involve regularly praying for one another's non-Christian friends and contacts. Many cells hold periodic social events to invite these non-Christian friends to. Of course if the cell is truly functioning as community through the week, then a newcomer may well know half the group on his first visit to a cell meeting.[3]

Here we need to debunk the myth that has proved a stumbling block to many seeking to apply cell church in the West. They have interpreted the emphasis on witness as meaning that a constant aim is to bring non-Christians 'cold' into the cell meeting. Leaders in New Zealand said that this understanding had largely led to the rejection of cell in a whole denomination, which concluded that cell was unrealistic and too big a challenge for existing home groups. However, think how Jesus did it in the Gospels. He built the community of the 12 by times spent alone with them. But he used their relationships with others (Matthew and his tax collector friends) and took them with him to the most natural social events *outside* the cell of the 12 (for a meal with tax collectors or with Simon the Pharisee) and built relationships for the gospel there. This is where Alpha can work so well with cell, as members of one or two cells run a course together and then bring converts back to their cell.

Of course, this will seem too highly structured for some tastes. But the 4 Ws are an outline, not a straitjacket. As Steve Croft, one of the pioneers of cell in the UK put it, 'Structures don't bring life. Only the Holy Spirit does.' The structures are only the fireplace; the Holy Spirit is the fire. And the best place for the fire is in the fireplace! Structures and Spirit are complementary – both are needed in a living cell.

Once the values have been internalised and appropriate practices and structures have aided their becoming a

---

3 Ralph Neighbour, *Where Do we Go from Here?* (Touch, 1990), 225. Neighbour's fourfold structure did not originally use the 4 Ws – these were named in his *The Shepherd's Guide* (Touch, 1994), 170.

way of life, cell-based church can fly! And that means trimming the set of the wings to the fluctuating winds and air currents of the surrounding culture. The direction of global society tends more and more towards individualisation and community breakdown at every level. Small-wing church as a place of belonging and counter-cultural discipleship, combined with large-wing church celebration, couldn't be more appropriate. Although highly challenging, it is what we were made for and such flight truly expresses the grace of the kingdom.

5

Church Planting with Cell Church

George Lings

I served in various churches for 8 years as a layperson, then for 22 more as a curate or vicar, but since 1997 I have worked for the Church Army as a researcher into emerging forms of church. I count it a gift from God to spend my time learning from the pioneers and being, so to speak, a watchman (Ezek. 33:2) who is bound to communicate what he thinks he observes. I love watching, comparing, connecting, trying to understand, and to put emerging conclusions in ways that will help others. One output flowing from my research is teaching church planting to evangelists in training. On the course we study cell church and compare its instincts with church planting ones.

Cell Planting and Church Planting Overlap

Both cells and plants claim to be church – even when either may not look much like it to outsiders. Like cells, church plants are Christian communities born to reproduce. Their genesis and goal is effective ongoing mission and evangelism by creating further new churches that will reach new people. And both are reproduced out of previous churches. Cells do not come from nowhere. Even when pioneers start them, they were members of previous churches. So the long-term vision of both cells and plants have powerful factors in common.

Parallel instincts for what church should be like

• Relationships in community constitute the vision of what church is meant to be. Both think church is essentially people, rather than buildings or ministers, and are prepared to be radical in order to get back to that.
• Evangelism is not just for specialists. In both, evangelism becomes the role for many members. So for a change, evangelists are reconciled with, and even valued by, the church!
• Ministry is for all, by all.
• Multiplication is normal. Decline or plateau is not healthy. Even addition is only second best. Health comes from giving away resources, so as to multiply.
• Diversity is welcome. Creativity not cloning, empowering not tight control, is the way.

Operate well together

• Work in a working-class or non-book setting where middle-sized church (50+ to 200) can be foreign to an oral, immediate culture. Larger congregational church tends to have a more complicated management structure, literary-based information dissemination, and a quasi-parliamentary decision-making process.
• Break through the 50 barrier in church size. Cell makes the unit size of church smaller, with each unit encouraged to grow. There is evidence that where the local

culture operates with extended family, then around 50 is the social maximum number. That leads to a small-congregation mentality, which needs radical change if there is to be growth. Cell makes the unit size of church much smaller, with each unit encouraged to grow.

- Assist in multiplying leaders. In cell more of the leader's time goes into recruiting, training and apprenticing leaders - and small groups are the ideal context to grow leaders. Growth and multiplication of leaders is the key human resource that will either enable or limit progress in both cell and planting.
- Simplify the church's inner life. One cry since the 1990s has been that churches are trying to do too much, including what isn't necessary, with members who have less time. Both cell and planting try to concentrate on what is essential and discard the rest.

Where Has it Happened?

In cell planting (as opposed to transforming existing churches) I see three interweaving patterns. It is not a simple matter of just starting cells. Every situation has both a context and history, which affects the choices and dynamics.

Church planting through cells

If this is done by independent churches, say in the New Church stream, this could be anywhere in terms of geography and social background. In practice it tends to be done in centres of population, to have enough people to recruit from – often, sadly, including other churches. Illustrations would be the birth of the Community Churches, meeting in varied venues in town centres, or the establishing of Fusion in several universities. Fusion, a cell-based arm of the New Churches, deliberately seeks to influence and win for Christ a share of the student population and create future leaders for their churches, just as in the past SCM and then IVF did (albeit using different methods) for the historic denominations.

If the plant has been sent out from the Church of England, a territory-based denomination, it can only happen where a clear hole in the system exists. Technically everybody falls within a parish, but in urban contexts there are housing estates where virtually nobody goes to church. Not only that, but in post-industrial areas the story has been one of alienation, not just separation, from institutional forms of church. A new starting point is needed to overcome the dominant view that 'church and Christianity are not for us'. It is thus no accident that two Church of England examples of church planting from scratch cited below occur in areas of local authority rented housing, and the third in an area of mixed social and private housing. They are deliberate mission choices to connect in ways that are distinct enough from past rejected models of being church. As such they tend to be pioneer plants, that is, those that identify and respond to a weakness that needs redressing. Consequently they start with slim resources and this affects how the work is done.

Roy Hollands is a Church Army officer who worked in Leicester from 1994 until 2000. Holy Apostles parish included a council estate built between the wars, from which few people came to church. When he arrived, a mission hall for the estate was on its last legs, spiritually and architecturally. After its planned death in 1997, Roy was asked to find a way forward. After research, he chose cell because it would not be seen as another unwelcome initiative from an outside institution, nor an equally fruitless call to 'come back to your parish church'.

It could work subversively and evangelistically within the local culture and could offer hands-on discipleship for new Christians, but done in a non-book way. He and his wife Ruth started by joining the five people in the only house group on the estate, and, after many months of prayer, talking and searching, three members decided to become cell for the estate and two moved out to a parish group. The cell members used the Willow Creek *Network Course* (Zondervan, 1994) to discover their gifts and the kind of church they were called to be. In finding further members, they looked for people who lived locally, felt called to the plant and wanted to demonstrate God's kingdom. Living Stones was launched as a cell plant in September 1998.

I am impressed that they adapt all the thinking and written material about cell to the local culture. For example, for some time the 'Word' section focused on relationships, priorities and money, using a course produced by Unlock called 'Go for it', which makes considerable use of film clips from *The Full Monty*. This stirred interest among the neighbours! Another example is that they use a twice-weekly pattern: one time gathering to pray and eat, and the other to do worship and word, rather than pack all 4 Ws into one meeting. In fact they hadn't heard of the 4 Ws until after they found their local format. They also spotted that the estate worked differently summer and winter. In summer people chatted over fences and in streets, while in winter they retreated to their houses. So food-based evangelism focused on the summer, while maturing and discipling became dominant in the winter. They made contacts and saw converts. As the initial cell contained a number of potential leaders they were able to move with some ease to two cells in June 1999. They then started a fortnightly cell for the leaders.

The measure of their success is an indigenous church, with lives being changed and a fringe of interested people being attracted. It is still small, with some 20 members, and is facing the challenge that Roy and Ruth have moved on to an equally demanding ministry in New Mexico, but it has made an excellent beginning on an estate where there is nothing else.

A similar story could be told about Martin and Sharon Garner, pioneering cell on a paramilitary estate in Lisburn, Northern Ireland. Given a free hand to develop a church on the Hill Hall estate, they started a cell in 1998, and doubled it in 1999.[1]

The challenge of both stories lies in the slim human resources with which they started, and the lack of indigenous leadership to take multiplication forward. I am sad that in the Lisburn case the sending church has withdrawn its support of the cell. I have seen, in some parts of the church nationally, an unwillingness to tolerate diversity and a quite unrealistic expectation that those won to a new form of church will also come to the old form. Our instinct to insist that people must 'come to us' is in painful contrast to the 'Go' direction shown us by Jesus in the Great Commission. Our assumption that they should become like us is equally flawed and is reminiscent of the Judaisers in New Testament days. It merits as much robust challenge as Paul gave to the Galatians. Cell, like other new forms of church, is prey to these reactionary forces. They represent a possible glass ceiling that may prevent cell becoming the force for the kingdom of God in the UK that it otherwise might be.

---

1 For the full account see my 'Has Church Reached its Cell Buy Date?' *Encounters on the Edge* 3 (Church Army, March 1999). Available from Church Army's Sheffield Centre (tel. 0114 272 7451).

Church planting alongside the congregational model

Some plant cells alongside a congregation because they feel that transforming an existing church is too long a task. They hear stories of the length of time it may take (seven to ten years!) for cell values to be truly adopted by the people, and all the structures to be appropriately overhauled. Some leaders assess it as too hard a task to overcome deep resistance to change without severe loss of membership, and yet at the same time the urgency for change from others seems compelling. So a new wine-skin is prepared for new wine, while keeping the old wine in existing containers. I would call this 'parallel planting'.

I do not know how often this has been done by other denominations. I guess the smaller and newer the church, and the more authoritarian the style of leadership, the more likely it is that wholesale transition will be implemented. In the Church of England I know of roughly 20 examples of transition, another 20 of moving to 'Meta Church' – a kind of halfway house to cell, but also about 10 examples of 'parallel cell plants'. It is striking that they occur in a very different social context from the plants from scratch. Most commonly they are in suburbs or towns. Here church membership is decided much more on the basis of mobility and choice, unlike church among the poor. Urban middle-class people go where there is provision for the needs of their families and to the style of worship and teaching from which they think they benefit. Providing cell here, and particularly in this way, is widening the nature of that choice and working with this increasingly influential dynamic, which is endemic in our consumer society. Michael Moynagh's *Changing World, Changing Church* (Monarch, 2001) offers a searching evaluation of this trend. Because of these factors, this kind of plant is more often a progression plant, that is, building on some strength. This starts with larger numbers and resources, which is very different from pioneering a plant from scratch.

A variant on this parallel route seems to be emerging in the synergy between cell and Alpha. It is eminently possible for a group of cells to put on an Alpha course as a reaping process, following the sowing done through relational evangelism, but it also is the case that members finishing an Alpha course may want to become the next cell. Indeed the fairly holistic character of Alpha, whose social cohesion comes through the food and small intimate group experience, shows it shares many cell values. There are now fresh straws in the wind that some Alpha converts may not be ready, or even want, to join a traditional model of church. The birth of a parallel cell-based church is one way to work with this understandable desire, and yet retain relationship between 'big wing' and 'small wing' church (see Chapter 3 in this volume).

Paul Bayes is the vicar of St Winifred's, Totton, Southampton. Totton was a village and has grown 40 per cent in 20 years to a town of 30,000. Its members look to Southampton for work, and to the sea or New Forest for leisure. Totton itself feels bypassed. The church was small but had earned goodwill. Called there in 1994, Paul and his wife Kate longed for more missionary effectiveness but they did not relish having to wait until it had slowly built up to a large church. Some positive small-group experience from his university chaplaincy days became allied to his encounter with cell thinking in 1997. At much the same time three couples from different places, all of whom placed a high value on small groups, joined the church. They became a cell church prototype of what would become All Saints Everywhere – a network church for all of Totton, based firmly on cell values.

I found Paul humbly and helpfully clear on important starting principles. Cell is about values not methods, and the latter will never be a substitute. Values are grasped intuitively and experientially, not academically and technically. So prototype is the ideal start – people actually doing cell. Cell is contagious rather than infectious, and certainly can't be caught out of a book. He is equally clear that a disciple's spirit of following is a better starting place than too much creativity. He feels we need to learn humbly from Asia and Africa where cell has been practised longer, and not bring in our sophisticated Western adaptations and qualifications, insisting that what happens in Singapore cannot occur in Southampton. When they meet, the shape and content is firmly directed by the 4 Ws and the particular order used at Faith Community Baptist Church.[2]

In keeping with this centrality of values a credit-card-sized list of cell values is given to prospective members only when they show they own them! So these believers no longer try to *teach* cell either to fringe people or to interested Christians – instead they *invite* them to come and see. After a time newcomers are visited to see whether cell values have taken root in them. The acid test is the extent to which members have espoused the 'Nothing competes with cell' value. It is a usefully equivocal phrase. It gives a priority to cell over any competing church demand; and it acts as a slogan that testifies to cell as daily bread, not cream cake, in the Christian life.

They have taken seriously the value to multiply, worked hard to ensure that the witness dimension was not squeezed out of meetings, and shaped their lives to

---

2 See their web site and the heading FCBC.

build natural links with others. Learning from Africa and Asia about faith expectancy permeates the process. Because it is a parallel church, new members have come from two sources: converts from the world and converts from the existing church.

They are serious about cell being Anglican – just as people of another denomination might be about it being Baptist or New Church. Alex Welby, in Hatherleigh, Exeter Diocese, has taken a similar 'parallel cell' route and writes attractively about being both Anglican and cell. Totton Christians talk of a 'family of congregations' of which All Saints Everywhere is one, with a name to match. The 'two-winged church' value naturally helps them to validate this, since they live in creative tension with a congregation-based church of which Paul is also vicar. From one cell in 1997 there are now five (soon to be six), two of which are intergenerational. They involve the lives of about 60 people of all ages. Clearly a new work is flourishing.

Cells for youth

It could be argued that this is not a separate strand at all, borne out by the fact that cells for youth have started in the two different ways cited above. I see this viewpoint, but am convinced that today's youth genuinely represents a different culture from the previous adult world. This is not the place to spell out differences between Millennials, Generation X and previous generations, nor to unpack the profound shifts from modernism to postmodernism. But what follows is that there has been such a cultural shift at the end of the twentieth century that ministry to youth represents a different mission field:

Young people are growing up in a different world to that experienced by previous generations. The life experience of young people in modern industrialised societies has changed quite significantly over the last two decades.[3]

If it is true that today's youth are a different culture, as people like Graham Cray argue, then the work of planting among them has even more significance because they will grow up to be adults with a different culture and will not grow into becoming more like the culture that the church has learned to reach.[4]

The primary frontier which needs to be crossed in mission to young people is not so much a generation gap as a profound change in culture.[5]

Youth is therefore a particular planting context and deserves distinct treatment. Within this third planting strand there are cases of starting cells among non-churched youth – such as the work of Liz West, who used to direct youth ministries for Youth With A Mission (YWAM) and now heads a cell-based church in the Harpenden area.

Or take the case of Steve Tennant in Deal, Kent. Steve was recruited by a consortium of churches in this small town. He began with street-detached youth work and school-based connections. Using cell principles they created from these links, and the conversions that resulted,

---

3 A. Furlong and F. Cartmel, *Young People and Social Change: Individualisation and Risk in Late Modernity* (Open University, 1997), 5.

4 George Lings, 'Eternity: The Beginning', *Encounters on the Edge* 4 (Church Army, November 1999), 23.

5 *Youth a Part: Youth Work in the Church of England*, Church of England report GS1203 (Church House, 1996), 2.11.

small groups for discipleship. In this case the process of planting – again in pioneer mode – began with evangelism and only later became more fully church in the sense of community and worship. The sad thing is that this work flourished, but began to be seen as church alongside but different from existing church. Then the local tensions arose about which denomination the new young Christians belonged to. I was reminded of an aspect of the worst colonial missionary scenarios, and our export of denominational barriers.

There are other stories such as St Alkmund's Derby, where existing youth work has been transformed to cell, with wonderful results in discipleship and outreach, though the adult membership remains congregational in values and identity.[6]

Summary

Cell touches places that other churches do not reach. It connects with mission contexts closed to the congregational church. Spiritually it sustains a vibrant ongoing and outgoing discipleship. These are priceless gains. Cell and planting can be good friends.

The ability to multiply leaders is both a potential strength and an Achilles heel of cell. It is really hard to reproduce a gifted new cell leader, because the longer-term elements – of life experience, solid biblical knowledge, pastoral wisdom and discernment – are not quickly acquired. This is particularly true when working in underclass contexts, where few or no positive models exist in the surrounding culture.

---

6 Bob Hopkins, *Cell Church Stories as Signs of Mission*, Grove Evangelism booklet 51 (Grove, 2000), 14–18, gives the details.

Some wonder whether cell can work in cultures where the home is used for family only and there is no culture of friends being invited in. My experience in a Sheffield church that transformed to cell suggests this can be worked around.

The examples we have seen show that churches of any denomination can go cell, not just the New Churches. Indeed I see fruitful dialogue between the theology of cell and that of historic churches to discern enduring values and outmoded forms.

Moreover I believe cell is a wonderful channel God can use, but is not the source of life itself. Its origins lie in churches that are already growing. We cannot bolt it on to dying ones and expect the same result.

6

Changing Church: The Story of a Transition

Chris Neal

This chapter comes with a clear government health warning. It is the story of one small part of God's church in one small corner of his world. It is the account of one church's journey from traditional church into cell. It is a story that, by no means complete, is still unfolding and that continues to raise as many questions as it answers.

The experience of transforming into cell church, sometimes confusing, but always exhilarating, has been and continues to be an untidy process. In the midst of all the discussion and exploration there has always been the confidence that God's Spirit is still at work, and that through his promptings we are moving into a new understanding of what it means to be the Lord's church at the beginning of the twenty-first century.

I hope that, by telling the story, the more technical issues explored by others elsewhere in this book can take flesh, and the reflections on the theological and practical implications offered here will encourage and help others to undertake a similar journey.

One of the great insights of the early church Luke gives us in Acts is that those first disciples learnt to do theology on the move. Being open to God was not simply responding to received wisdom from the past, but learning to hear his word and Spirit in the vortex of life. If we have learnt nothing else over the past few years, we have learnt that the Lord is constantly calling us to move forward with him.

Not Just Another Bus to Catch

Reflecting on some 30 years of ordained ministry within the Church of England, and having been part of the Christian scene for some 10 years before that, it becomes ever clearer that the Church of England (and indeed the Church *in* England) has been waiting for the one 'good idea' that will reverse years of decline.

Christians in Western Europe are now living at the end of a period of retrenchment that has continued for some 150 years, and that has been accelerating since the end of the Second World War. It is hardly surprising then that the prevailing ethos is so frequently one of deprivation and the management of decline; in so many parts of the church maintaining the little we have has become the main purpose in life.

Over the past 40 years various theological insights and new methodologies have been trumpeted as the panacea to halt and then reverse the decline. From charismatic renewal to liturgical reform, from church-growth principles to seeker services, they have paraded before us like a line of London buses, but each in turn has failed to deliver.

This is not to say that each has not had important insights. Indeed many of these movements and moments have been gifts from God. However, they have all addressed a symptom rather than tackling the root cause of the problem. It would seem that God is radically and fundamentally wanting to change how we understand his calling to be his people, how we engage with his missionary heart and reconnect with a broken and hurting world.

To understand cell church as another 'quick fix' will miss the point completely. Someone recently said we often pray for revival while God is actually in the process of resurrection. The task before us is not to revivify what was appropriate for previous generations, but to discover the new resurrection life to which God's Spirit is calling us. God's one desire is to have his people equipped and living in such a way that they can readily and effectively make known his love and grace to a confused and confusing culture.

Thame by Name and Tame by Nature?

The story is set in Thame, a small medieval market town, 15 miles east of Oxford in central England. With a population of 3,000 for several hundred years, the town saw rapid expansion in the 1980s to some 12,000 people. Could this sleepy, rural middle England town become a seedbed for church growth and transformation?

The town's history was not encouraging. The story (probably apocryphal) is told that when Wesley visited he could make no significant spiritual impact and left declaring it was 'Thame by name and tame by nature'. What is certain is that it was the only town in England to petition against the coming of the railway (in the 1800s) and against the installation of mains drainage (in the early 1900s).

However, against this unpromising background, the church did see steady growth from the mid-1980s and throughout the 1990s. The adult membership of 168 in 1986 had grown to some 500 by 1999 and a significant ministry had also been developed among children and young people. This growth had been encouraged by a community-focused mission strategy, together with church planting and the development of a variety of seeker groups and a programme of seeker services.

The early 1990s saw a radical reordering of the medieval church building, equipping it for ministry and mission at the turn of the millennium. A new congregation had been planted in 1994 into a primary school, and 1998 saw the multiplication of congregations meeting in the parish church building. Each of these congregations had a discrete ministry/leadership team and there was a network of house groups. These met fortnightly, were loosely linked to congregational life and were equipped with study materials. There was, however, little expectation of the membership, nor indeed the positive valuing of membership.

Seeing the Vision and Setting the Course

At one level all seemed well. People were coming to a living faith in Jesus Christ and lives were being transformed by his Holy Spirit. Further, a significant number of people were being called into new spheres of ministry, both in the UK and overseas.

However, by 1997 there was a growing seed of restlessness and dissatisfaction. (With hindsight this now appears to have been God-given, though it was uncomfortable at the time.) Growth plateaued at 500 and even began to decline. People were still coming into God's kingdom, but others, seemingly established Christians, began slipping away. Discipling and mentoring were becoming difficult, if not impossible.

The beginning of a new beginning

In the autumn of 1997 the Staff Team withdrew for one of their twice yearly 'Away Days' (72 hours to pray, think, plan and grow together in community). On this occasion the team began to share and explore their concerns for the situation and during this time God began to open eyes to new things. The thinking and work of those three days were summarised by three statements. These have become seminal in the journey.

There was a recognition that things could not continue as they were and the dissatisfaction was summed up in the following phrases. There was a determination to move from

- grind to gifting;
- programme to people;
- organisation to organism.

There was an honest recognition that the way church was 'being done' simply ground people down, laying increasingly heavy burdens upon them. Although paying lip service to every-member ministry, God's gifts were not being released in any significant way.

It was also recognised that because of the size of the church, and because of the predominance of the congregational model, church life revolved around programmes. This seemed the only feasible and sustainable way to function, but it meant that people were being used to feed the programme, rather than a programme being the servant of people.

All this meant a complicated organisational structure, leaving little or no room for the organic or the spontaneous.

Daring to think

It may have seemed a long time in coming! Surely a chapter on transition from traditional church to cell church should immediately have 'cut to the quick' and clearly and concisely laid out the principles and values? In the abstract and theoretical – yes, it should be like that, but God calls us to live in the real world, dealing with real people. If the church is truly an organism living in the power of the Spirit, then it will be in the process of living, and in the relationships people share, that God's way will be given life.

If cell church is simply seen in terms of organisation and structure, then we are immediately back into the old inherited mindset, and cell will simply become a 'bolt on' to what is already happening and will be treated like another 'quick fix' panacea.

The experience in Thame suggests the journey, the process, is as important as the destination. One of the great biblical truths is that of pilgrimage – it runs throughout the Old and New Testaments. Peoples and individuals learnt to walk with the living God and discover his purposes and plan. This was certainly the experience of the disciples and the model Jesus has left us. This sense of journey is echoed in the Acts of the Apostles as the early church found itself blown into every culture and every corner by the wind and fire of the Spirit.

The Staff Team in Thame began to realise (and continue to do so) that the exploration of cell church was not simply a pragmatic exercise to maintain church growth, but was a deep challenge to their understanding of what it means to be God's church, how this can be expressed in a contemporary situation and how the imperatives for mission and evangelism are worked out.

Transition to cell is not primarily a transition of *doing*, but a fundamental transition of *being*. It means putting on an entirely new thinking 'cap' and venturing out into new possibilities. Some will find this frightening and, indeed, threatening. Others will discover exhilaration and step out, risking everything in the confident belief and trust that the Lord is with them.

The start of the journey

The Staff Away Days in the autumn of 1997 proved to be a defining moment. As the three criteria were formed, discussed and explored, the team began to see that cell church principles might well speak to the situation being faced. Cell was a shadowy, emerging possibility in the minds of some of those present. Some had been to cell conferences, most had begun to read around the subject and all were excited by cell theology and thinking.

By the end of the Away Days there was a commitment to research as thoroughly as possible. This process would also include talking to the congregational ministry teams and house group leaders and, with them, discuss the possibilities and implications of moving into a cell church mindset. In hindsight, although this was thought to be a good and thorough preparation, this phase needed much more shaping and leadership than it received. This was not neglected through lack of interest or commitment, but because there was little recognition of the radical nature of what we were about. This continued and continues to be a key issue – changing a mindset is a long-term process.

Further Away Days were held in March 1998 and by this point there was a growing sense of anticipation that the Lord was about to lead us into a new adventure of faith. People reflected on their reading and thinking. A good number across the congregations seemed ready to move into cell. There was a growing conviction that as a staff team we were at a point where a commitment to leadership in this direction could and should be made.

The most significant decision from this time was to appoint a staff team member with responsibility for the transition process. In the providence of God's timing we were at a staff change point and needed a further stipendiary member. Although that staff member would have responsibility for two congregations it was felt he or she could also oversee the transition. Again, with hindsight, this was an unreasonable expectation, but at least it showed the beginnings of a recognition that the transition process required gifted and committed leadership.

This need has become more and more apparent as the journey has unfolded, but God has been gracious in his provision of the right people just as they have been needed.

Following these decisions David Jackson was appointed to the staff team in May 1998 and he took up his post in September that year; his job specification clearly stated his oversight of the transition, and David willingly and ably began the task. The scene was set for what looked like a simple transition into cell church. In reality the roller-coaster ride was only just beginning!

Preparing for Transition

With the decision to transform to cell things began to move apace. During the autumn of 1998 David Jackson settled into the staff team and began a period of preparation. Training was organised and materials written. It was decided to move into a cellular under-standing of church in Lent 1999. As the process unfolded, three major areas had to be faced.

Evolution or revolution?

This was a primary decision. How should transition be handled, given that there was a large church with multiple congregations in inherited mode? Should the existing house groups be closed down and new groups formed along cell principles, or should the groups be allowed to transform themselves into a new way of being? After much discussion the 'evolution' rather than 'revolution' route was chosen. It was felt, probably correctly, that to move in an arbitrary way would alienate people, produce much heat but little light, and create an enormous pastoral workload.

Closely linked with this decision was the choice of name for the groups. Cell had been explored, tentatively, some 12 years earlier. People had reacted violently to the word 'cell' – thinking it either imprisoning or subversive and Marxist. Hence there was still concern over the language used and the name 'HomeBase' came into use. The rationale was that it was a place where you could be at home and grow in discipleship, and a base from which you could engage in mission and evangelism.

Finding the core values

All who were committed to cell church saw the impor-tance of explaining the model, laying the foundations and teaching the core values. Bill Beckham's book *The Second Reformation* (TOUCH, 1997) had made a great impact on many people and the two-winged bird became (and continues to be) a central motif. After discussion and prayer the Great Commandment and the Great Commission were seen as foundational and 5Ms were adopted to express the core values:

• Magnify
• Membership
• Maturity
• Ministry
• Mission

Over the months a further M was added to these core values:

• Multiplication

During the autumn of 1998 and the early months of 1999 these principles and values were taught and preached. This was at a congregational level and through the house group network.

Training and preparation

Alongside the general teaching, house group leaders, together with others who showed leadership potential, were invited to take part in a training course. This explored cell church principles and tried to demonstrate the difference between cell and house groups. There was also an attempt to help existing leaders understand how to transform their house group into a HomeBase.

All this preparation culminated in a Team Conference in February 1999. Cell was to be launched the following week.

We Have Lift-off, Possibly

If we had expected to stand back and watch the two-winged bird soar we were to be sorely disappointed. A year on and it had to be admitted there was little defining difference in church life. Some groups had grasped the principles and were beginning to live and work in a different way. Others, particularly old house groups, could not understand what all the fuss was about and continued to do things as they had always done them. For others, congregational life continued as it had done for the past 400 years, and small groups remained the choice of the enthusiastic few.

However, in the midst of this rather gloomy picture there was a continuing conviction that God had called us on this journey. The picture of the two-winged bird, the primacy of the small group as the place of belonging, still excited many people and there was no sense of wanting to give up. During these somewhat frustrating months, two significant things happened.

First, three of us, somewhat ironically, were invited to teach cell church principles at the Church Army Training College in Nairobi. Obviously something hit home because the following year, as a result of the Nairobi trip, we were invited to the refugee camps in northern Tanzania. Some 300 pastors living and working in the camps were eager to learn and apply cell principles in their ministry.

Both these opportunities were immensely humbling. As we taught we came to realise how little we had actually allowed the biblical principles of cell church to change our mindset. We recognised the deep entrenchment of the old thinking patterns and the radical transformation that needed to take place. However, on each occasion we returned ever more determined to continue the journey and get it right.

The second significant event occurred in the summer of 2000. Unexpectedly David Jackson had to return to the United States to care for his aging mother. This seemed a body blow. He had brought a clear vision of cell and was ably helping us through the transition process. However, in his graciousness the Lord was about to provide the next important link in the chain.

Beginning Again

On to the scene came Steve and Diane Eyre. Steve had come to faith in his teens through the ministry of Bob and Mary Hopkins. He had kept in touch with them, had heard them speak, and both he and Diane were passionately on fire for cell church. Steve, having time available and clearly gifted in leadership and strategic planning, joined the Staff Team. As a couple, they are now heading up the small-group network and overseeing the continuing transition process.

From this watershed the past months have seen a period of steady growth and development. The foundational principles and core values have been revisited and, I trust, strengthened and reinforced. The 6Ms now provide the bedrock of our purpose as church and are being discussed and owned by the councils and ministry teams. Those cells that are beginning to fly have received encouragement and support. A process of training and shaping for the new mindset has been unfolding during the course of the year. This autumn (2001) sees further development of the support and training network together with the launch of 'Foundations for Life' – a discipleship course that the small groups are being asked to trial for future use with new

Christians. It is written around the 6Ms and will again underline the principles by which we want to live and grow.

Reflections

This story has been told in an impressionistic way and much more depth could be added. The story though has been a huge and fast learning curve for the church in Thame – and it continues to be so!

In the process of changing a traditional church into one living by cell principles, the fundamental mistake was rushed and limited preparation. All the literature had warned against this. The prototyping of a group and gradual transition had all been highlighted. Like many before us, we ignored the warnings and the advice and so had to start again and move forward on a firmer footing.

However, the experience of transition also raises further fundamental issues:

1. *The focus on congregation.* The past three years have shown how congregationally focused the church is. Because that is the received model from centuries of experience, it is hard to break into a new model. This is as true for those deeply committed to the process as for those who are more wary.
2. *Being church.* Closely linked to the former comes the constant challenge to understand what it means to be the people of God. For most this is still defined by meeting on a special day, in a special place and expecting special people to do special things. Cell breaks through this straitjacket and enables the exploration of church in new and vibrant ways.

3. *The primacy of mission and evangelism.* While many would acknowledge this, in reality most church members find it hard, if not impossible, to make the link between church and the rest of life. Cell challenges this divide and encourages people to see life as a whole.

4. *Gifting and ministry.* To see people discover their God-given gift and find their place of service is a great privilege. Cell gives so much more opportunity for this to happen.

5. *Creativity, imagination and excellence.* So much of what is done as church is second-rate and poor. However, as people engage with each other and God's Spirit within small groups, they can touch the creative and imaginative heart of God. This can have immediate and immense 'spin-offs' both into the gathering as congregation, and also into the wider community.

6. *Living in a new mindset.* Certainly transition to cell means putting on a new thinking cap. Moving into a new mindset is like moving into a new house. Some of your old furniture may come with you, but it will be in different surroundings, so will look and feel different – and might even be put to new uses. Cell is the challenge to move into a new mindset, or maybe regain the one God always intended. It is also important to recognise that the culture in which we live is now living in a new paradigm. With the wider culture's questioning and desire for exploration, its longing for reality, search for relationships and community, its suspicion of hierarchy and institution, being the people of God in the small and big wing gives opportunity to reconnect with those around us.

7. *On being Anglican.* Cell will raise huge questions for those in an Anglican setting. It will challenge our understanding of the role of the ordained, the place of communion and where and how mission takes root.

But these questions are and will be asked anyway. They are crucial to our understanding of God's purpose for his church in this generation. Far from being a threat, cell can provide the rigorous critique and offer the model and framework for the way forward.

Finally

Despite all the problems and setbacks, the last three years have been an amazing testimony to God's goodness and graciousness. Despite all our mistakes and misunderstandings new Christians have been birthed, lives changed and discipleship deepened. Three groups have multiplied, several are on the verge of doing so and for many others the possibility of the kingdom growing is firmly on the agenda.

We are living on a building site. It is untidy, chaotic, and for many, confusing. There is, though, the belief that the Lord is the architect and we are trying to build according to his plan. Changing the metaphor, we long for a two-winged bird that will fly in the power of God's Spirit, engage lovingly and creatively with a broken world, and demonstrate the reality, vibrancy, authenticity and integrity of God's kingdom.

The story continues . . .

7

Breaking the Barriers

Albert Vun

> What are you, O mighty mountain? Before Zerubbabel you
> will become level ground. Then he will bring out the cap-
> stone to shouts of 'God bless it! God bless it!' (Zech. 4:7)

The church faces all kinds of barriers. Barriers of tradition,
prejudice, disobedience, division and unforgiveness, to
name but a few. These must be overcome if the church is
to advance. And, in my experience, the cell church has
spectacularly helped that advance.

Transition to cell church begins with the assumption
that it is God's will for the church to grow and to be fruitful
in all her ministries. Jesus said, 'I am the true vine, and my
Father is the gardener. He cuts off every branch in me that
bears no fruit, while every branch that does bear fruit he
prunes so that it will be even more fruitful' (John 15:1–2).
Even fruitful branches need pruning if there is to be more
fruit. The church is never to rest content with a low level of
fruitfulness. The fast-changing environment around us
and the constant challenge of God's living word warn
us against becoming fossilised in an institution that ties us
down with cumbersome rules and regulations that hinder

mission. Almost every great enterprise of evangelism and church growth begins by challenging, and then changing, existing assumptions of what church is about. Think of the Acts of the Apostles. Think of the Reformation. Remember the great missionary movements. Then there is the recent charismatic renewal that has swept across the denominations. Change is painful, but it is necessary. The gospel in its essence requires barriers to be broken.

In 1990 I was appointed by our diocesan bishop, the present Archbishop Yong Ping Chung, to be the rector of St Patrick's parish, Tawau, a small town in the south-eastern corner of Sabah (formerly North Borneo). It is a border town, with Indonesia to the south and the Philippines towards the east. The church was already large by Anglican standards, with an English-speaking, a Chinese-speaking and a Malay-speaking congregation. The overall attendance then was about 600 every Sunday. The church had a total of 12 Bible study groups. Some of the groups had existed for over ten years. As a student in Singapore, as well as in England, I had grown up with Bible study and discipleship groups. So I encouraged the home Bible study groups and wanted to build upon this strong foundation. However, I noticed that the church did not have a working strategy for evangelism. So in my second year, together with a few leaders, I began training people to do evangelism by visiting. We had considerable success. Nurture groups were started to teach the new believers their new-found faith, while at the same time preparing them for baptism. Most of the nurture groups were taught by me, since I was the only pastor. At the end of each batch, I would assign the newly baptised believers to our Bible study groups. Soon, I was disturbed to discover two clear trends. The home Bible study groups proved ineffective at nurturing the new Christians, and the groups themselves lacked any evangelistic dimension. I spent some time

praying and searching. That was when I was introduced to
the idea of cell church. Years ago, while in college, I had
read about the cell groups in Korea. I thought these were
the same as home Bible study groups, only known by a
different name. But as I struggled with a church that was
already strong in the word of God, but not structured for
effective evangelism and discipleship, I discovered that
cell is a whole new way of looking at church.

This discovery transformed not just my ministry and
leadership, but also my theology of church. The change
required a massive paradigm shift. Cell church is not just
another method of church organisation: it is a new way of
seeing, experiencing, and working out the life of a local
church. Since then, in the past seven years St Patrick's has
grown from a Sunday attendance of about 600 to 3,000.
At least seven new congregations have been planted.
The giving of the church has multiplied nearly tenfold.
We have just over 400 cell groups, whose leaders are
monitored by zone pastors. The journey of transition has
brought about effectiveness in evangelism, ministry, and
in equipping of leaders for the new cell groups that are
added every month. Looking back, we had to overcome
several major barriers. Other churches have also
attempted to launch into cell church, but some of them
experienced only limited success because they were
unable to overcome one or more of those barriers. Others
have failed in their transition altogether. So, what are some
of these barriers that must be overcome?

Breaking the Barrier of Tradition

Today's practices become tomorrow's traditions. Therefore, there is no way we can avoid having traditions.
Traditions are not bad things, and we need them to

provide stability and continuity. But often churches exalt traditions to such a position that they dominate the life of the church. As a result, the church becomes irrelevant to the community where she was supposed to bear witness. The cell church is very different. It decentralises the ministries of the church to the cell groups, which meet in homes. In a sense, the cell, meeting in a home, *is* the church. So the emphasis is not on buildings or on programmes. All the facilities of the church are mobilised to assist the cells to be successful in two simple agendas: the cell must *minister*, and the cell must *multiply*.

This may set the cell church in direct conflict with the established church along with its set traditions and buildings. The fact is, most of our buildings are built to last, and having very old buildings gives the impression that the church is antiquated. Can we function in the buildings of past centuries and still be powerfully effective in the present generation? If we cannot, it is because we make the denominational traditions sacred, and the church buildings become places for tourists to visit and admire. The church is no longer seen to serve the present generation, and it fails to bring people to Christ.

In cell church, the focus is totally on the faith serving the people. All its activities are there to serve the spiritual needs of the church, to help it reach out into the community to express the love of God and win others to Christ.

So when St Patrick's moved into cells, the whole life of the church was transformed. Our worship services came alive. Gone was undue emphasis on denominational traditions like the Prayer Book or the distinction between the clergy and the laity. We were in danger of falling into 'worshipping our ways of worship' rather than worshipping God! Some churches are so engrossed in keeping the right form that they are no longer sensitive to the worship needs of the new generation. No wonder many so-called traditional churches lose their young people. Church traditions, Prayer Book, the liturgy, and denominational distinctions are all necessary and good. But they are not to be regarded as sacred. This barrier of traditionalism must be overcome, and cell church enables it to happen.

Breaking the Barrier of Leadership

John Maxwell says, 'Change the leader, change the organisation. Everything rises and falls on leadership! Unchanged leaders equal unchanged organisations.'[1] This is true in secular organisations. It is equally true in the church. To change the direction of a local church, either another leader has to take over, or the existing leadership has to undergo change.

Some of the obstacles to implementing cell church that arise from the leadership are as follows:

1. *No agreement in the leadership.* To make any change effective, the agreement of the key leaders is essential. The pastor needs to pray and work for this agreement. This is especially critical at the early stage of transition. There will be resistance. Yet change will not come without resistance. If the vision can be taught, shared clearly, concisely and completely, agreement can come.

I was blessed by a group of six men who prayed with me every Monday lunch hour in the earlier years of our transition. They had invited me to join their prayer meeting when I first arrived at St Patrick's. After two years of meeting almost every Monday for fellowship and

---

1   John Maxwell, *Developing the Leader within You* (Nelson Word, 1993), 49.

prayer, this group of leaders understood my heart even though they did not always agree with me. When I began to make changes towards transition into a cell church, at a time when many church members misunderstood me, this group of leaders supported me. They helped to communicate the vision. They also helped to harness the unity of other leaders. On several pivotal occasions, they helped build bridges between me and those who had initially opposed me or dragged their feet.

2. *Fear of change.* We tend to settle into our own patterns where we find comfort and security. Change, especially in the practice of religion, is always difficult. People resist it. But growth involves the willingness to make changes. The church can either settle down or move on. If the church is on a journey, there will inevitably be movement and changes along the way. In cell church radical change is inevitable.

For one thing the organisational structure needs to change. We used to have over 20 committees running the different ministries, like Women's Fellowship, Young Adult Fellowship, the various Sunday Schools, the Boys' Brigade, the Girls' Brigade, the visitation ministry, the hospitality ministry, the building committee, the Church Council, the school boards, and so on. Because of the different language groups, the number of committees was multiplied threefold. The rector of the church was expected to be the adviser in all the church committees. An active member of the church would be involved in two or three committees. Imagine the paperwork produced by all these committees. Imagine the exhaustion of the rector! If each committee met once a month, there would be at least ten committee meetings a week. So members of the church were very involved in activities but ineffective in ministry.

But in a cell church all the ministries of the church are mobilised in the cells. The functions of the full-time pastoral staff of the church are to serve, support, supervise and equip cell leaders and members to be effective in ministry and evangelism.

So a church must be willing to make changes to her organisational structure. We had to ask ourselves whether we wanted a youth fellowship or to restructure the youth ministry into many self-multiplying youth cell groups. Some churches want to have cell groups but also keep everything else because of the unwillingness to dismantle existing structures. This inevitably leads to more and more activism, and the cell groups become an additional ministry on top of the already overloaded weekly activities of an active local church. This will guarantee failure.

3. *Blockage by strong individuals*. In every church, there will be some influential leaders. Many of them will have been there longer than the senior pastor. Often unconsciously, some of these leaders take on themselves the role of preserving the 'heritage' of that local church. If the pastor or rector plans to introduce any new ministry, it can be approved only if several of these strong individuals give their permission. So through teaching and leadership skills, these strong individuals must be won over before there can be successful implementation of cell church. If this barrier is not overcome it causes much pain as a result of conflict between the pastor and key lay leaders.

4. *No strong mandate*. Any major change made to an existing church must be based on a strong mandate. This mandate has to come from hearing from the Lord. When we implemented transition from an established Anglican

church into cell church, what little I knew about cell groups came from reading books written about a large church in Korea. At that time I did not know of the cell church movement that was already happening in places like Singapore. In the three months of waiting on the Lord, asking why our church seemed unable to assimilate new believers into our Bible study ministries, I became convinced that we must restructure the church so that evangelism and ongoing discipleship became the backbone ministries of the whole church and not the ministry of one department. It was then that I was introduced to cell church. Only after the Lord had convicted my heart did I begin looking out to learn from what others were already doing. I still remember being accused of jumping on to the cell church bandwagon in the early years of our transition. That was not true for us. We had sensed a deep conviction and mandate for change before we looked at other churches and learned from them. This is a necessary factor for successful transition because we cannot copy another church's vision. We may learn from those who have developed certain ministries successfully, but the conviction for such a radical change must be from above. Otherwise the pastor may not have the spiritual authority to endure the journey of transition.

5. *Ignorance about authority*. Some churches do not allow their pastors to have the authority to lead the church. Of course spiritual authority may be abused and many pastors have been guilty of such misconduct. Even so, the senior pastor must be given authority to exercise leadership, without which the work of the church cannot be carried out. The people cannot be mobilised effectively. A leader can only be effective if he has authority to lead. When we lack the will to do something, we often resort to forming committees. We justify this by saying that this is

'dispersed authority'. The problem is that the authority is so dispersed and shared that no one really takes responsibility for the work and growth of the church. We have too many church committees that withhold authority from key leaders, paralysing the church and preventing her from getting into creative and cutting-edge enterprise. Someone once said, 'A committee is a group of the unqualified appointed by the unwilling to do the unnecessary.' Successful cell church leadership requires letting the senior pastor exercise rightful authority to get the job done.

6. *Failure to maintain focus.* After a vehicle is set in motion, it is not only necessary to keep it on track but also to keep it going. I have seen some pastors who started on the transition journey but failed to maintain momentum. Often it was because they had not committed enough energy to the task. We can do many things and yet achieve little. But if we focus our energy and effort on what is our priority, we will be able to achieve much. Once the church is committed to cell church, the whole body must focus effort to build up the cells and train the leaders. Persistence and constancy of purpose is necessary for success.

7. *Unwillingness to mobilise resources.* Jesus in his parable spoke about how one servant 'dug a hole in the ground and hid his master's money' (Matt. 25:18). He did not use it to profit the kingdom. Many churches or leaders of churches fall into a spiritual condition where they would rather deposit the church money in the bank than see themselves as stewards to mobilise their resources to extend God's kingdom – for training, for mission, for raising up leaders, for works of kindness and other 'profitable' works of the church. They consider

themselves as guardians of the church funds and facilities rather than as stewards who are to manage effectively the resources the Master has placed in their hands. Often we end up in church council meetings debating over small amounts of money because of people who have buried the talents God has given to the church. In Jesus' parable, the root cause of this spiritual condition was a wrong view of God: 'Then the man who had received the one talent came. "Master," he said, "I knew that you are a hard man, harvesting where you have not sown and gathering where you have not scattered seed"' (Matt. 25:24).

The root problem is this: people who think they are careful with money but in reality are the 'lazy and wicked' servants. They know that when they allow the resources of the church to be mobilised, they themselves must also work! I thank God for St Patrick's church council where all the council members are cell leaders, supervisors or zone pastors. Not only do they own the vision of the church, they are committed to mobilise resources to make the ministries and mission of the church effective. In the last seven years the church has been instrumental in planting or starting seven new congregations, both locally, and farther away. When the church is willing to mobilise what God has given us, it will become effective both locally and globally.

Breaking the Barrier of Numerical Growth

And He Himself gave some to be apostles, some prophets, some evangelists, and some pastors and teachers, for the equipping of the saints for the work of ministry, for the edifying of the body of Christ. (Eph. 4:11–12 NKJV)

Church growth experts have long observed how a church grows to a certain size and then, before reaching the peak, the growth rate slows and the church plateaus or even declines. Some people put the barrier at around 200. Looking at the Anglican churches in Malaysia, over 90 per cent of the congregations have fewer than 200 adults in one sitting on a typical Sunday. This is after over 100 years of work. Some churches with multiple language congregations may have a total Sunday attendance of over 200, but the attendance per congregation will still be below 200. For many years people have wondered why this is so.

The answer is that the ministry of the church lies in the hands of the clergy. Because of the clear distinction between the clergy and the people, in the way we dress or in the way we are addressed, the clergy, rather than the people, are seen to be the ministers. The people are not encouraged to use their gifts to minister to one another. The structure of ministry in a typical Anglican church continues to perpetuate this one-person 'ordained' concept of ministry. Cell church, however, deliberately places the responsibility of ministry and evangelism in the cells. The ordained and full-time pastoral staff can then concentrate their efforts on equipping church members to minister in the cell groups. I used to be called on to do most of the home blessings, to visit and pray for the sick, to counsel members, and to visit the homes of lapsed members. Now, most of these pastoral ministries are done by the cell groups, led by trained cell leaders. We had known this as a theory for many years, but we were only able to implement it effectively when the church transformed into cell church. The pastoral ministries of the church are no longer limited to one person or to a small team of pastors.

Breaking the Barrier of Boundaries

As an Anglican church, we had inherited the idea that most church work is done within the church building. We used to think of church planting in terms of raising new buildings first, and then moving some members there to start a service. The rate of church planting was limited by our ability to build new buildings. This is based on the wrong idea that we must have a church building before a church can function. Inevitably it promotes the idea that evangelism and ministry must happen within the church compound. Cell church moves the church out into the community. In fact, the more ministry and evangelism happens outside the church compound, the better. We see every cell group functioning as a church in the homes. The size and the effectiveness of the church are not limited by the building. It is like having a church 'without walls'. Initially, adult groups met in the homes. Later, even our youth groups moved out from the church compound into homes and schools. We even have some of our youth cells meeting in the homes of parents who are unbelievers. This puts the church into the community, making our members function more effectively as the light of the world and salt of the earth. They are able to respond to the needs in their neighbourhoods. Every cell is challenged to claim the neighbourhood for Christ. Several times a year the cell groups go out to pray around the neighbourhood. They visit homes in their areas to proclaim the message of Christmas by singing carols. We no longer sing carols in our own members' homes because every cell group is out there singing in the homes of those who as yet do not know the meaning of Christmas.

For a lot of established churches, the journey of transition into cell church is a difficult one. I know of pastors who have resigned because they failed to lead their churches to the desired change. Nevertheless, transition to cell church can be an exciting journey of faith and growth. Barriers can be broken.

By wisdom a house is built,
    and through understanding it is established (Prov. 24:3).

8

Cell Church: Theologically Sound?

Graham Tomlin

It may work, but is it right? Very often in the past, evangelism and church-building have been approached in a task-oriented and functional way. The argument goes 'if it succeeds in getting people into church, then surely it can't be wrong?' A moment's reflection will expose the flaws in this way of thinking – cash handouts and free beer every Sunday might also draw the crowds, but would hardly be an authentically Christian way of doing church. The theological question can't be avoided: cell church may have proved an effective means of planting and growing churches, but in going down this line, are we compromising something essential of what it means to be Christian? Have we gained success, but lost the gospel in the process?

It's worth pursuing the question a little further before we start looking at an answer. In part, the question asks about the biblical basis for cell church. For a particular approach to church to be authentically Christian, it needs to show that it is at least in harmony with the church as the New Testament represents it. This is, of course, not hard to demonstrate. It seems clear that the New Testament church was organised along some kind of small-group or house-church lines, as confirmed by the frequent references to meeting in homes in the book of Acts, and the churches that met in the houses of such early Christian hosts as Priscilla and Aquila (Rom. 16:35; 1 Cor. 16:19) or Nympha in Laodicea (Col. 4:15). In passing, it's intriguing to note the way Paul refers to these gatherings: he calls them 'the church in their house'. These are not secondary subgroups of the church or a voluntary gathering of the superkeen: they are the true church itself. The New Testament evidence has been well covered elsewhere and won't be repeated here – it simply confirms that some form of small-group gathering, based in a home yet related to the wider church in a city or region, played a central role in church life in the cities of the Roman Empire.[1]

However, there is a further dimension to this question than simple biblical proof-texts. It might be argued that even though the New Testament church was organised with small home-sized churches as its basic unit, cultural conditions are different today and we needn't necessarily adopt this as a model for church any more than we insist on women covering their heads or men greeting one another with holy kisses on Sunday mornings. The more fundamental question concerns how far this way of being church coheres with a wider biblical and systematic theology. Is this way of doing church authentically Christian?

According to the letter to the Ephesians, God's purposes for the world are tied up, amazingly enough, with the

---

1 See R. Banks, *Paul's Idea of Community: The Early House Churches in their Cultural Setting* (Hendrickson, 1994); V. Branick, *The House Churches in the Writings of Paul* (Michael Glazier, 1989). R. Banks, *Going to Church in the First Century: An Eyewitness Account* (Christian Books, 1994), gives a fascinating account of what an early Christian meeting might have felt like.

church. His intention throughout history has been that 'through the church, the manifold wisdom of God should be made known' (Eph. 3:10). The 'wisdom of God' is of course a complex and evocative phrase within the Bible, but it carries a sense of the nature, grace and character of God himself. When we think about cell church, there is a basic question we must ask: How far does cell church make known the wisdom of God? How well does it express the character and nature of the God to whom the church belongs? Or perhaps more fairly, does it do these things better than more traditional ways of being church?

As awareness of the multifaith nature of western society has grown over the past 50 years, intense interest has grown in two doctrines with a particularly strong claim to identifying distinctively *Christian* theology from other forms. They are the doctrines of the Trinity and of the cross of Christ. In a short chapter such as this it is clearly impossible to provide an overall account of the theological coherence of cell church. In what follows, however, the aim is to measure cell church against the contours of at least these two fundamental ideas to begin to establish how genuinely Christian it is.

Cell Church and the Trinity

In recent theology, the doctrine of the Trinity has increasingly come into focus as the distinctively Christian approach to the doctrine of God. If we are to ask who the Christian God is, and how he is different from all the 'gods', the answer must be that he is the one revealed to us as Father, Son and Holy Spirit. The American Lutheran theologian Robert Jenson in particular has insisted that the Trinity identifies the God we are speaking about – it is the name by which we know him.[2] Other theologians have lamented the fact that the Trinity was not generally used in early Christian theology to help understand the nature of the church. Colin Gunton suggests that as a result, the early church quickly became a hierarchical and authoritarian institution rather than a true community of the people of God. Gunton is one of several contemporary theologians[3] who suggests that the Trinity should provide the basic model for the church: 'the church is called to be the kind of reality at a finite level that God is in eternity'.[4] For these theologians, the doctrine of the Trinity tells us that God's essential nature is *communion*. In other words, God is not a solitary figure sitting in divine isolation and self-sufficiency, but instead is a kind of community of different persons, united in love and shared identity.

It used to be commonly thought that the doctrine of the Trinity was a bit of Greek metaphysics concocted by early church theologians, obscuring a much simpler view of God presented in the Bible. Now it is increasingly recognised that the Trinity, while not explicitly described in the pages of the New Testament, is the only way we can do justice to the God revealed in Jesus Christ. The God who created the world and remains distinct and transcendent over it, yet who also appeared in human form on the streets of Palestine, and who now enables ordinary sinful people to respond to him from their hearts, can't be described in the simplistic terms of divine singularity. As Karl Rahner insisted, God's inner nature is revealed in the way he has

---

2 R. Jenson, *The Triune Identity: God According to the Gospel* (Fortress, 1982).

3 See also J.D. Zizioulas, *Being as Communion: Studies in Personhood and the Church* (Darton, Longman & Todd, 1985).

4 C. Gunton, *The Promise of Trinitarian Theology* (T. & T. Clark, 1997), 80.

revealed himself in Christ and the Spirit.[5] The Trinity is not just a convenient way of speaking about God's way of doing things: it tells us what God is like in himself. If God really is Trinity, then he is not a single self-sufficient individual, standing outside all relationship. Instead, he embodies relationship and community in his very being. If so, this has important implications for the Christian life, which too is not to be lived in individualist isolation, but has to involve relationship. The church is meant to reflect God in being primarily a community of persons united in love, rather than a rigid hierarchy or a list of individuals who have no relationship.

These theological emphases are helpful and suggestive. However, sometimes in theological discussion of the Trinity, it is possible to slip into one of two traps. On the one hand, talk of the church as reflecting the internal life of God is all very well, but does it work in practice? The church is not a theological abstraction dreamed up in lecture halls, but is a collection of imperfect people trying to follow Christ together in the pressures of modern life. How can local churches begin to reflect this Trinitarian nature of God? And what will it mean anyway? A further problem is that the Trinity can seem like an exclusive club. Some writings on the subject convey the impression of the persons of the Trinity absorbed in mutual contemplation, with little interest in anything outside themselves. This is a static, inward-looking understanding of God, and probably leads to static, inward-looking churches as well!

To take the last issue first, the answer to this static view of God is to reassert the importance of the Trinity as a missionary doctrine. In other words, the unity of the three

---

5 This is the essential meaning of Rahner's famous dictum 'the economic Trinity is the immanent Trinity and vice versa' (K. Rahner, *The Trinity* [Burns & Oates, 1970], 22).

persons is not found in their mutual absorption, but in
their outward focus. John 14 pictures both the Son of God
and the Holy Spirit being 'sent' by the Father (vv. 24, 26).
The focus is not upon internal contemplation, but on a
mission to reconcile creation to God. Gregory of Nyssa,
one of the key figures in the development of the doctrine
of the Trinity in the early church, used to insist that it was
a mistake to think of the persons of the Trinity having
separate jobs to do, so that the Father's job is to create, the
Son's to redeem, and the Spirit's to indwell. Instead, everything God does has a threefold character, so that in
creation, for example, the Father creates through Christ the
Word, and the Spirit broods over the void (Gen. 1:1–3;
Col. 1:16). In other words, the unity of God is found not in
internal self-congratulation but in action, in his work
in creation, redemption and bringing everything to final
glory. If we can put it this way, God's Trinitarian being is
not so much centripetal (centring in upon himself) as
centrifugal, always moving outwards in love and energy
towards his creation. The Trinity has a strong communal
bond – different persons held together by a common
identity and mutual love. At the same time, however, this
is no inward-looking community, absorbed purely in its
own welfare, but rather the Trinitarian God longs and
loves to draw others into his own life and into communion
with himself.

To move back to the former of our two questions: How
can the church be like this in practice? This is where cell
church begins to score highly. The emphasis of this way
of practising church lies firmly on two interlocking
themes – community and evangelism. Because of the
intimacy that becomes possible due to their smaller size,
the emphasis placed upon sharing one another's lives,
and the importance given to the small group as the basic
unit of church life, cells have a greater capacity to create

genuine and effective community than many other models of church life. There is a level of mutual care and involvement in the lives of others in cell-based church life that is simply not possible in the more distant relationships established in a church focused primarily on larger congregational gatherings. At the same time, cell church theory places a strong imperative on the function of the cells to multiply as well as minister. In most cell churches, evangelism and care for outsiders are named as among the key purposes of the cell, in contrast to 'home groups' where the focus tends to be exclusively internal, on Bible study and mutual pastoral care. In many cell churches it is precisely the sense of intimate community, the warmth of a group committed to accepting and caring for one another, made possible by a deep sense of being bound together in God's love in Christ that attracts and holds outsiders, leading towards the cell's multiplication into further cells. Here is a model of church life that seems to combine precisely the same strong bonds of community with a centrifugal outward-looking focus, which finds its expression in effective outreach, as we have noticed within the Trinitarian life of God himself.

Cell Church and the Cross

The other theme mentioned earlier as particularly distinctive to a Christian understanding of God was the doctrine of the cross. By this is meant not so much the idea of the cross as the means by which God brings about the forgiveness of sins (usually called the 'atonement') but the idea that something unique about the Christian God is revealed in the cross of Christ. A comparison with Islam is perhaps helpful at this point. Islam has a fairly simple view of revelation. God reveals himself in the divine text of the Koran, mediated through the prophet Muhammad. God is not personally involved with the world, revealing himself within it, much less allowing himself to be crucified at the hands of sinful people. This scandalous and startling claim is one that Christian theology makes: in Christ, it is God himself who is reconciling the world to himself (2 Cor. 5:19). In Christ, God himself suffers the devastating consequences of human sin.[6]

The result is a very different understanding of God. Paul reminds the Corinthians that God achieved the salvation of the world through the last thing they would have thought of: the execution of the Messiah on a Roman cross. Just as God worked salvation through a weak, suffering Messiah, so he still achieves his purposes through a weak, unimpressive apostle and socially inferior people, rather than the social or educational elite of Corinth (1 Cor. 1:18–31). For him, however, the cross does not remain a past event, locked away in history as the means by which salvation was won, and of no continuing relevance for present Christian life. Instead, it must decisively shape the way church works now.

The cross therefore represents the characteristic pattern of God's work in the world. He works his purposes through what the rest of the world regards as weakness rather than strength, foolishness rather than wisdom. If all this is true, then the Corinthian Christians' squabbling over who is the most eloquent speaker, who has the most impressive spiritual gifts, and in particular the snobbishness of the richer members of the church

---

6 For the development of some of the ideas in this section, see G.S. Tomlin, *The Power of the Cross: Theology and the Death of Christ in Paul, Luther and Pascal* (Paternoster, 1999).

towards the poorer ones are completely out of place.[7] For Paul, this 'theology of the cross' insists that power and influence is used in a distinctively Christian way. He invites the richer Christians to give up their rights to eat separately from the poorer Christians, or to go to pagan dinners parties, which are offensive to their less affluent Christian brothers and sisters. A Christian use of power is to give it away – to surrender rights and privileges for the sake of others.

Since St Paul, a number of others have taken up this theme. Among them, Martin Luther used a powerful exposition of the theology of the cross to oppose the abusive late medieval papacy. More recently, Jürgen Moltmann is perhaps the most important contemporary expositor of this theme in his seminal book *The Crucified God*.[8]

The use and abuse of power is increasingly seen as one of the key questions facing Christian theology today. The case against Christianity argues that it became the dominant religion of the Western world not because it was more true but because it was more powerful than its pagan rivals. The Christian church's record in the use of power is not exactly spotless when we remember past scandals of crusades against Muslims and heretics, and more recent abuse of children and ethnic minorities. Contemporary postmodern people are much more sensitised than previous generations to power games and how they operate, and are likely to pick up much more quickly when power is abused by those in authority, whether teachers, doctors, politicians or priests.

---

7 See 1 Cor. 11:20–2. See also G. Theissen, *The Social Setting of Pauline Christianity* (T. & T. Clark, 1982), 145–74.

8 J. Moltmann, *The Crucified God* (SCM, 1974). See also E. Jungel, *God as the Mystery of the World* (T. & T. Clark, 1993).

God, the most powerful being in the universe, achieves the most difficult thing in that universe – the redemption of sinful humanity – through the weakness of the cross. He exercises power by surrendering it out of love for his creation. As we saw above, if the church is to 'make known God's wisdom', it will need to reflect in its own life the nature of God himself. This will mean the kind of outward-looking community life we noticed in the Trinity. It will also mean a community marked by this same surrender of power and 'rights', and that exercises power through love.

Churches can often seem the last bastion of hierarchical power. Clergy often still dominate, and if not, powerful groups of lay people can wield power from the centre, whether it be (in the Anglican Church) through the PCC or the deacons' meeting. Decades of talk about 'enabling' or 'every-member ministry' have still not dislodged from many churches the concentration of power and responsibility in the clergy. It is not always the clergy's fault: often church members want the vicar or minister to play this kind of role, and refuse to let it be any different. The result is a depressing catalogue of clergy burnout and lay frustration.

One of the features of cell church is its strongly decentralised structure of power. Rather than one clergyman at the centre deciding all, dispensing all pastoral care, teaching and sacraments, the cell structure devolves power and responsibility to the level of the small group in a much more radical way than the older 'home group' system, where home groups are effectively a secondary activity, mainly for the especially committed, but definitely subordinate to the main congregational gathering, which of course is presided over by the clergy. In the cell church, power is effectively 'given away'. It is, in one sense, a much more risky strategy. Clergy at the centre are no longer seen as the indispensable heart of the church, pulling all the strings (and many clergy breathe a sigh of relief!). The cell leader is genuinely given far-reaching responsibility for the church meeting in his or her home. At the same time, even within the cell itself, the emphasis is not upon the leader as teacher and dispenser of wisdom and guidance. Instead, the accent lies on mutual learning, ministry to one another, and a sense that no one in the church is to be a passive, powerless recipient, but rather an active giver and receiver of care and Christian advice. The cell *is* the church – it is the primary place where church happens, where pastoral care is exercised, where practical learning and application of scriptural teaching to real life takes place, and where evangelism occurs. Here the clergy may provide a framework and some theological expertise, but there is a much stronger sense that power is dispersed among the whole church than in most instances of more traditional church life.

It is clear to many observers of cell church that here lies a much more devolved and balanced distribution of power than in many more traditional churches. It is a notion of power better equipped to answer postmodern concerns about the abuse of power and truth than the authoritarian models of power operating in many of those traditional churches. More importantly, it reflects the understanding of power seen in the cross of Christ, where God surrenders his own power to allow others to be drawn into fellowship with him.

A Note of Caution

These two doctrines do, however, have some cautionary notes to sound to those seeking to operate their church on a cell structure. The doctrine of the Trinity speaks not only of outward-looking community, but also of interdependence. One danger in cell church is that in encouraging cells to take responsibility for themselves they can develop a life of their own, regarding themselves as separate from or even superior to the rest of the church. Rogue cells, which start behaving in random ways in the human body, have a name – cancer. The Trinitarian nature of God recalls the church to community; it also recalls it to unity and interdependence.

Likewise, the theology of the cross, and its implications for a Christian use of power, has important things to say to cell churches. Some cell churches, despite the dispersion of power to the cells, can develop highly authoritarian structures. They can be overly directive and limit individual initiative. Clearly a balance is required here. To avoid the chaotic disharmony that comes when every cell does what is right in its own eyes, there has to be a common direction for the cells in a church. At the same time, the critique of abusive power in Paul's theology of the cross cautions against cell church leaders wanting to determine too tightly what each cell will do and look like. Cells will be different, just as people differ, and leadership is all about providing a framework within which life can grow, rather than forcing it to happen.

On these two counts at least, cell church is perhaps not just another gimmick, the latest quick-fix to church growth. It is a way of being church that is not only biblically prefigured, but theologically responsible. It can claim to represent and reflect the nature of God in more distinct and effective ways than churches that offer little intimate community or care for the rest of creation, or that are modelled on strongly centralised notions of power. It is thus not without its dangers and temptations, but it offers an exciting and authentically Christian way of gathering church that deserves more, not less, theological reflection.

9

Cell Church: Culturally Appropriate?

Rob Merchant

'But of course, it can't work in our culture!' Maybe I am naive, but I was amazed at how often I heard this reply after a study trip to Malaysia. It had brought me into contact with cell churches and had left me excited about the possible applications of the cell church model. I was reflecting about these sceptical replies, each predicated upon cultural inappropriateness, with a Malaysian friend who is a cell church pastor. He observed that when cell church was introduced from the USA to Singapore, people in Singapore said, 'It won't work here: culturally it's American.' When cell church was introduced from Singapore into Malaysia, people responded, 'It won't work here: culturally it's Singaporean.' And when cell church ideas were taken back from Singapore to the USA, some folk said, 'It won't work here: culturally it's too Singaporean.'

Yet cell church as a model has worked and does work, as the above observation shows, in many different countries each containing very different cultures, but still we become concerned about the issue of culture as we ask, 'Will it work?' Perhaps it is that the cell church model poses such challenges to our methods of leading, discipling, growing and simply being church, that in a desperate need to dismiss such a challenge many people view the issue of 'culture' as the safe fall-back answer that will halt such radical ideas as cell church.

Contributors have already outlined models of cell church, a theological analysis and places in which it has been applied. I will not be revisiting such themes in this chapter. My concern is simply to ask, 'Before we dismiss cell church from our own culture as irrelevant or unworkable, do we actually understand what our own culture is?' In unpacking something of what culture is, and the influences of culture upon people today, I hope to demonstrate why cell church must be given serious consideration as a potential tool for church structure, discipleship, and for effectively communicating the gospel through words and action in a rapidly changing world. It is not the only way of 'being' or 'doing' church, but it is a model that could benefit significant numbers of churches.

What Is Culture?

The word 'culture' is used today with tremendous enthusiasm, and a variety of meanings can be attached to it. People talk of 'consumer culture' and 'popular culture'. Some speak of 'national cultures', others of 'local' or 'ethnic' cultures. There can be a 'culture of leadership' or a 'cultural identity', while social commentators have developed the idea of 'subcultures' that coexist within cultures. In all these variations upon a theme, what is certain is that you can be left with a bewildering array of terminology and the feeling that you are no closer to understanding culture than when you began.

The difficulty is that when we speak about the impact of culture we are under the influence of the culture to which we belong.[1] Culture is not a value-neutral experience. Lesslie Newbigin observed that there is no such thing as 'culture-neutral' theology.[2] Writing this chapter I am speaking from my own cultural experience and identity, into your own. You may agree with my interpretation, you may consider it to be invalid in your experience. You may not see the relevance or its application for your own locality. Quite simply, whatever we try to do we cannot escape the impact of culture in all its forms.[3]

Surprisingly, this bewildering array of possibilities is a great place from which to start! If we can acknowledge that the communities in which we live contain multiple forms and expressions of cultures, and that even in receiving or giving information we are influenced by those cultures, directly or indirectly, then we can escape the danger of thinking of culture in monochrome terms.

One of the benefits of the postmodern critique in the West has been to unearth the diversity that exists in our societies, showing culture to be a gloriously technicoloured experience. But this poses problems. Many church leaders and members have developed during a period in which they were told that modernity ruled and that there was such a thing as a cultural norm. No wonder such people regard cell church as culturally inappropriate: within a monochrome understanding of culture it would be, because it stands in direct contrast to traditional forms of church.

---

1 H. Montefiore, *The Gospel and Contemporary Culture* (Mowbray, 1993), 2.

2 L. Newbigin, 'Culture and Theology', in A.E. McGrath (ed.), *The Blackwell Encyclopedia of Modern Christian Thought* (Blackwell, 1999), 98–100.

3 H.R. Niebuhr, *Christ and Culture* (Faber & Faber, 1952), 51.

However, in the communities in which we live and worship, technicolour rules. If someone objects, 'But culturally . . .' they should be asked, 'But what culture?' Is this your local culture, the perceived culture, popular or national cultures, ethnic culture? Or are you using 'culture' in an economic or social structure or class sense? Are you talking about the culture of your church, or the culture of your denomination or network? Is it your experience of a culture of leadership, or is it simply your own culture? There is nothing simple about 'culture', and there are no clearly defined manuals from which the facts of a culture may be read. Cultures are complex entities that have to be pieced together. To assume there must be a pre-existing coherence is to assume wrongly.[4]

If we write off cell church as culturally inappropriate we show that we misunderstand the complexity of 'culture'. The key is to begin by recognising the many cultures in which we live and worship, both inside and outside the church, and then to see how we might apply the basic ingredients of cell church, which seem to have a remarkable ability to transcend national boundaries when applied to local contexts that contain great diversity.

Culturally Relevant

Globally our societies are changing. It is hardly 'breaking news' that the impact of an interconnected world reaches into all kinds of places. During a recent trip into the interior of Sabah, Malaysia, an area that I naively supposed would be worlds away from UK cultural influences, I met supporters of UK football clubs, who

---

4 N. Couldry, *Inside Culture* (Sage, 2000), 103.

proudly wore the football strip of 'their' team, and owners of DVD players and widescreen TVs powered by generators: they were watching the latest films! There are no longer technical barriers to prevent cultural influences of one country reaching another thousands of miles away. People engage with this new world. They are well aware not only of their own cultures but of many others, which they constantly draw upon as they form their identities.

However, while there is growing interconnectedness in society at large, recent surveys have highlighted the increasing disconnection of society and church in the UK.[5] The same trends are apparent in the USA and Australia. For many years 'secularisation theory' has been put forward as the reason why, ever since the impact of the Enlightenment, society and religion have supposedly become increasingly estranged.[6] But secularisation theory itself has come under increasing scrutiny in recent years, and its fundamentals are now called into serious question. Some commentators[7] looking at the impact of the post-1950 world have started to provide a more secure analysis, in which they recognise that technical, familial, societal, and economic movements of seismic proportions have brought us to our present state.

There isn't space in this short chapter to develop a full analysis of recent societal changes. However, I would like to draw out two key trends that I believe are globally

---

5 See the results of a significant UK survey by the Christian Research Association in P. Brierley, *The Tide Is Running Out* (Christian Research, 2000).

6 See David Martin's classic text *A General Theory of Secularisation* (Basil Blackwell, 1978).

7 See C.G. Brown, *The Death of Christian Britain* (Routledge, 2001). A superb thought-provoking analysis. The theory of secularisation has also been critiqued by writers such as Peter Berger and Grace Davie.

applicable and to which the cell church model could offer a significant response. They are *individualisation* and *customisation*.

First, individualisation. The sociologist Zygmunt Bauman has recently drawn attention to the fact that people are becoming 'increasingly individualised individuals'.[8] Bauman asks 'why the stories we tell nowadays and are willing to listen to rarely, if ever, reach beyond the narrow and painstakingly fenced-off enclosure of the private and the "subjective self"?'[9]

Second, we find the trend of customisation, which has been described as the 'second consumer revolution', whereby businesses are increasingly tailoring products to suit the demands of individuals or groups of customers.[10] We need only consider the supermarket loyalty card schemes in the UK, which are able to track our purchases and identify special offers that would suit us. Or think of the Internet bookshops, which track our purchase patterns and then make specific book recommendations the next time we log on to their site. The impact of such a consumer revolution highlights and reinforces the growing individualisation of society.

These two key trends combine to represent the two aspects of the individual's life, the private and the public sphere, deeply interconnected and deeply disconnected from the models of church presently deployed. You may consider these to be gross generalisations as you think of individuals you know who do not fit these supposed 'trends'. They do not take refuge in that remote private sphere, own a loyalty card or shop on the Internet. However, in that very process of identifying your individuals

---

8 Z. Bauman, *The Individualized Society* (Polity, 2001), 13.

9 Ibid. 12.

10 M. Moynagh, *Changing World, Changing Church* (Monarch, 2001), 19.

you are yourself participating in the individualisation of society, as the individual defines and enables your response.

Michael Moynagh identifies the issue as he explores the way in which churches have retained the sense of a 'one size fits all' mindset of what church should be. He observes, 'The church could get away with it in mass society, but in an it-must-fit-me world it won't wash anymore.'[11] Changing patterns of living bring new pressures and demands, and we increasingly face the idea of the 24-hour society. But where in a 24-hour society is there space for church? Certainly not through fixed meeting times on one day of the week. The model of cell church provides the potential by which a local church can be culturally relevant to the working lives of those who surround it and who live in the community.

Further, a variety of work cultures can already be found within a single church. There are those who work full time or part time, those who work in different sectors, people who are unable to work because they cannot find work or because their work takes place within the home, or people who have retired, willingly or unwillingly. Each group, and the list is far from exhaustive, faces different demands at different times in different ways. However, many churches insist on meeting at the same time and in the same way, simply because that has been the monochrome culture of the church!

If we fight to keep our traditional structure and method of church, we are fighting against the changing tides of culture, and present statistics suggest we are losing the battle rapidly. I am not suggesting that the Christian faith is going to disappear – not at all. But I can foresee the collapse of those denominations that do not begin to

---

11 Ibid. 33.

release local churches from national methodologies and allow them to explore, reaching into their communities in ways that meet people in their cultural spaces. Of course, the reader in Africa, Latin America or South-East Asia may think the Western demise is far from their own cultural situations. However, with the critique of a supposedly Western phenomenon – secularisation theory – as the cause of religious decline in the West, comes the implication that those forces that have affected the West are also affecting the rest of the world. Such is the growth of the individualistic society through the global interconnectedness of cultures and the global forces that influence them.

Cell Church: Culturally Responsive

Before discussing in detail the potential that the model of cell church holds in being culturally responsive, there is one final argument held up against cell church that needs to be confronted. Some commentators have offered the view that cell church is all about *control*: that its structure of cell pastors, cell supervisors, senior pastor, fivefold format, all have the impact of standardising and brainwashing its members. One person recently described cell church as 'a tool that may owe more to Lenin and Mao . . . Possible recruits are targeted, befriended, coerced with kindness, and then, and only then, seduced by the gospel.'[12]

Having witnessed cell churches in action, I find such comments incredible, as they turn what is a model of church into a 'monster', to be defeated at all costs.

---

12 John Chynchen, 'Kind Coercion to Conversion', in the *Church Times*, 6 July 2001. Chynchen's comments were made in the context of a review of Michael Green's 2001 book *Asian Tigers for Christ* (SPCK, 2001).

Admittedly control and the abuse of power can occur in the cell model, but it can also take place in the traditional parish model. The problem is not the model but leaders and their culture of leadership. Such resistance also arises when people perceive cell church to be a standardised product that insists on the application of rigid components. However, is this view of the 'product' (cell church) correct? Are we prepared to suggest that the culture of the cell church model is so strong that it can override all other cultural influences of age, community, status, history, identity, ethnicity, etc?

I would say no. I am a member of the Anglican Church, a Church that over the last couple of centuries has had a strong history of sending out missionaries, particularly in association with the development of trading partnerships and empire. These early Anglican missionaries took with them their own culture of 'church' and began applying this in a variety of national and ethnic contexts. However, when we pause and look at Africa and South-East Asia today we do not see lots of mini-versions of your average English Anglican church. Rather, we see African and Asian members of the Anglican Church who, while sharing many structures and forms of worship, have developed their own culturally relevant theologies, patterns of church and leadership. Anglicanism was shaped by the cultures into which it was applied. Many writers on cultural studies have pointed out that we must not underestimate the ability of cultures to adapt imported material for 'local' use.[13] To think the same is not true of the cell church, and so to regard it as some kind of culture-crushing beast – is at least mistaken and at worst a complete failure to understand the impact of our own local cultures.

---

13 Couldry, *Inside Culture*, 97.

Churches are made up of people who shape the church, bringing to it their own cultures and experience. And this is one of the cell church's greatest strengths: it has tremendous potential to be responsive to people. Consider for a moment. In the cell church 'church' takes place in the small group; worship, discipleship, evangelism, encouragement and care, all take place at the level of immediate relationship. There is no single minister attempting to care for all the members of the church and the local community: there are many ministers, each working with small groups of people. Once the group becomes too large for that effective one-to-one relationship, the group multiplies so that it remains a manageable size and relationship remains possible.

During my travels through the Diocese of Sabah I was able to witness the two principal aspects of the cell church, to *minister* and to *multiply*, in action. It was amazing and humbling to see people growing in relationship to one another and to Jesus in the cell group setting. When I went to Sabah I was suspicious of cell church, loaded as I was with my own cultural preconceptions. But I came to the liberating recognition that each cell group was different. Yes, they followed a common pattern of worship, but don't most churches who are part of the same denomination or network? But the cell group was made up of people and the people shaped the cell church.

I identified earlier the two key trends individualisation and customisation. It was exciting to see how one of the churches that had completed its transition to a cell church structure, St Patrick's in Tawau, Sabah, embodied both trends.

Because the cell is a small group, the individual is more easily recognised and valued. There is no one-size-fits-all mentality, so the need to conform to the culture and structure of a larger church is removed. Moreover, each cell had its own character, and not all cells met in the same way. While the adult cells met in people's homes, this wasn't culturally appropriate for the cells containing older people. Many older people lived with their families and their culture of 'church attendance' was to meet at the church building. Therefore the 'senior members cells' met together in the church building for the first part of their cell programme. They then divided into their cell groups for fellowship, returning later to the larger group, and finishing with afternoon tea. St Patrick's took the core aspects of the cell church model and applied it into its own cultural context.

Responding to the trend of customisation, each week cell group leaders would fill out a feedback form detailing their cell group's developments, needs and whether or not programmes offered by the central church leadership (e.g weekly teaching, ice-breakers, worship) were effective for that cell group. This weekly piece of market research meant that the central leadership were able to tailor courses and be responsive to the needs of the cell church. My lesson from St Patrick's was the possibility of engaging successfully as a church within today's individualised society in culturally relevant ways that valued and recognised individuals while bringing them into the body of Christ.

The UK theologian John Drane has made some shrewd observations from research both in the US and the UK. He highlights the way in which today's generations are people on a spiritual journey: they want to grow through the discovery of personal truths and practices, and they maintain that this growth takes place primarily through deeper relationships. Examining results from a major UK survey he observes that 'unchurched people are more interested in relationships than in receiving information about God or church . . . they are looking for relevance, not history . . . wanting practical answers to life's hard questions'.[14] The lesson of St Patrick's is that cell church has the potential to meet these needs and reach those outside the church, enabling them to start and continue their journey with Jesus.

Yes it Could Work. But Is it Right?

We need to ask a final question: Is it right to engage with cultural change to the level that we alter our structures of church to do so? Don Carson asks this question in the context of evangelicalism: 'To what extent has evangelicalism, in its attempt to influence surrounding culture, been so drastically shaped by that culture that it is in danger of selling its biblical and theological heritage for a mess of a pottage of perceived culture?'[15]

There is indeed a danger that we can become so culturally aware, desire to be so relevant that our theology, our doctrine, becomes shaped by the culture in which we live rather than by Scripture. The difficulty I find with some cell church proponents is the extent to which they move cell from being a model of church to being almost a model of theology. However, being culturally relevant in delivery and method is thoroughly scriptural. In the ministry of Jesus we see disciples of diverse cultural backgrounds, parables that are delivered in culturally relevant ways according to the situation of the hearers, and culturally diverse people groups responding to the good news of the kingdom of God. The apostle Paul took great pains to be culturally relevant (1 Cor. 9:19–23) and showed it in his

---

14 J. Drane, *Cultural Change and Biblical Faith* (Paternoster, 2001).

15 D. Carson and J.D. Woodbridge (eds.), *God and Culture* (Paternoster, 1993). See preface for quote.

address at the Areopagus in Athens (Acts 17). Cultural relevance is vital for the mission of church. We are not talking about content but method, and cell church is a method by which this mission can be carried forwards today, meeting people in their own cultural experiences.

Richard Niebuhr's conclusions on culture are as relevant today as they were in the 1950s:

> In his single-minded direction toward God, Christ leads men away from the temporality and pluralism of culture. In its concern for the conservation of the many values of the past, culture rejects the Christ who bids men rely on grace. Yet the Son of God is himself a child of religious culture, and sends his disciples to tend his lambs and sheep, who cannot be guarded without cultural work.[16]

I have found cell church to be a way of engaging within contemporary cultures that can lead people into relationship with Jesus and so away from the cultures that had previously held them captive. There will be people who will claim, despite the arguments advanced here, that the use of cell church is tantamount to the 'MacDonaldisation' of the church. They will continue to state the need to maintain our traditional structures and our norms of church culture because this has spoken to people in the past, so that in a world where there is an amazing fluidity of cultures the church needs to retain a monotone culture. However, let us be clear: these are not the arguments of engagement but the excuses of inaction. My hope is that such voices of resistance may dare to look around and see that it is they who have become culturally inappropriate.

---

16 Niebuhr, *Christ and Culture*, 53.

10

Cell Church: Its Strengths and Dangers

Michael Green

I am delighted at the variety and experience of the authors in this book. Graham Tomlin, an Oxford academic; Bob Hopkins and George Lings, church planters; Chris Neal, Diocesan Missioner; Mark Francisco, a Canadian cell pioneer; Bill Beckham, the doyen of cell church writers and a practitioner in Taiwan and in America; Rob Merchant, a sociologist-turned-curate; Albert Vun, an archdeacon from Malaysia; and Moses Tay, the recently retired Archbishop of South-East Asia – all come together from three continents to commend cell as a dynamic way of being church in today's society. So as we end this book, let us rehearse its strengths and its dangers.

Idea of Cell Church

Cell church is not some new fad. It stretches right back to New Testament days, when the Christians had no special buildings to meet in and no fixed liturgy to use.

Believers informally crowded into homes to worship the Lord, to read letters from the apostles, to pray, to break bread together, to enjoy fellowship, and to renew their passion for evangelism. At times they were able to bring a number of these home churches together for a large gathering, but large gatherings worried Roman emperors, so those occasions must have been few and far between. The main form of the church was unquestionably the cell in the home.

Bill Beckham has shown that this strand of informal home fellowship never died out, but it became increasingly marginalised down the centuries, particularly after Christianity became the religion of the empire in the fourth century under Constantine. Bob Hopkins has pointed out that it may not have been quite as serious as Bill Beckham supposes: some of the functions of the small group remained and have been widely used in the historic churches. But Beckham's main point stands – the bird of Christ's church was designed by the good Lord to fly with two wings, the small group and the large gathering. The latter has prevailed, and the small intentional gathering of Christians has largely disappeared. So church people intuitively see church as something they *go to* rather than something they *are*. And that inevitably leads to formalism, to concentration on buildings, to the prevalence of organisation over spontaneity and to clerical control. None of those characteristics appeals to the postmodern age in which we live. People do not like being organised by others. They are not drawn to authority figures. They much prefer homes to communal buildings, and they want opportunity for spontaneous relationships rather than being regulated by the traditional church. The decline of the historic churches underlines these considerations. It is time for change. And the cell is one of the most exciting forms of church being rediscovered.

Let us be quite clear what we are talking about. In cell church philosophy, a church does not *have* cells: it *is* cell. It is actually a far cry from the church home group. The home group usually stays much the same in numbers and membership: the cell church is in business to divide and multiply. The home group do not see their leader as a pastor: that is the vicar's job. In the cell, however, the cell leader is the pastor. The home group exists for companionship, prayer and instruction from the Bible. So do cells, but they evangelise enthusiastically (something rare in home groups) and they take seriously mutual ministry and accountability. Home groups normally exist for the enthusiasts. In a cell church everyone is a member of a cell. And whereas home Bible study groups exist alongside all the other programmes and organisations in the church, in cell church all these things disappear. The cell is everything. It is not about programmes but people. The aim is first to win them, then to build them up and turn them into leaders and missionaries.

So there is an enormous conceptual difference between home groups and cells. This particularly applies to the clergy. They had been used, in a traditional church, to doing almost all the teaching, visiting, planning and pastoral work of the church. In cell church many of these tasks are taken over by the cell and its leader. So the main task of the pastor is to train, train and train. It is his responsibility to 'equip the saints for the work of service, to build up the body of Christ'. And the body of Christ works through its cells. The cell visits members who are ill. The cell loves and holds its members accountable. The cell does the evangelism. The cell does much of the training, and its leader may well be involved in assisting the vicar at baptism and communion. I know churches where it is the cell leader who buries and marries people, even if the form is signed by the pastor! So it is no small thing to transform into cell mode: it is radical. It involves an entirely fresh mindset among clergy and people alike. That is why many find it too difficult a barrier to overcome. So some do not attempt it. Others begin enthusiastically, but cannot keep it up. Others fail because they attempt a compromise: they try to cultivate cells while also continuing all the programme-based life of the church. The result is exhaustion all round and the collapse of the experiment. It cannot be emphasised too strongly that if you are going to go cell, you go in for it boots and all! It is an entirely different way of being church. There is no halfway house.

Dangers of Cell Church

A glance at the previous paragraph will show what a dangerous enterprise cell church is. It requires a whole-hearted acceptance by the pastor, the lay leaders and the members of the church if they are to move in this direction. That is not easy to achieve. It will require much prayer, loving discussions, often one to one. It will require the patience of Job if the traditional mindset is to be changed. And it will require sacrifice by the pastor as he transfers many of his traditional functions into the hands of cell leaders who may well do them much worse!

Quite apart from this difficulty, which is harder for traditional churches than for the New Churches, who may well decide to start operations in cells, there are several specific dangers in the transition to cell church.

An obvious one is the upkeep of the church building: it may become neglected. But that can readily be overcome. The cell members will all be in the main building on a Sunday and, anyway, the old Fabric Committee can, with skill, be turned into a cell. Mark Francisco explains how this took place in one of the churches where he served: indeed, two of that Fabric Committee were converted during the transition!

Another danger is that cells may be thought odd, almost a cult, by the surrounding neighbourhood. This suspicion can soon be put to rest if the cells invite neighbours to occasional celebrations, and if there is plenty of friendship evangelism, for which the cell is ideally suited.

More serious danger concerns the leadership of cells. Albert Vun is an expert in training leaders for his 400-plus cells, but we are not all Albert Vuns. Not every ordained minister is a gifted trainer, and if he is not, there is serious danger of poorly trained leaders being put in overall charge of a dozen or so members of the congregation. Damage can be minimised by regular sessions between the pastor and the cell group leaders, but it remains a genuine danger, and every effort must be made to give cell leaders continuous and careful training, to avoid burnout and to maintain harmony.

Graham Tomlin put his finger on two dangers, and showed the theological antidote to them. There is a perennial danger of independence among cell leaders: with centrifugal force the cells can easily spin off and do their own thing. Graham shows from the doctrine of the Trinity that while there is diversity in the Godhead it is held together in unity. Unity in diversity is the model for Christian relationships and is crucial in the organisation of cells. Albert Vun insists on a practical way of ensuring this: the aims of the cell must be identical with those of the church at large. Graham also drew attention to the danger of authoritarianism that can be found in some cell leaders. The power and responsibility goes to their heads. But Jesus, though possessing all power, willingly submitted to his Father in utter obedience, even to death on the cross. That is the ground from which the lovely plant of submission should grow in all Christian leadership. Again Albert Vun comes up with an important principle, neglect of which causes chaos. The authority of the senior pastor in a cell church must be acknowledged and reinforced by the whole congregation and all the cell leaders. If he uses his authority gently and wisely the church will flourish, as Albert's has. If he is authoritarian and expects obedience without consultation, the church will collapse.

So there are undoubted dangers, particularly in the relationship of the cell leaders to the pastor of the church. One could enlarge on these. For one thing, there may not be enough suitable cell leaders to staff the cells. For another, they may not be well enough trained. A bishop in South-East Asia mentioned to me his main misgiving about cells: the leaders have not had the theological and biblical training nor the spiritual formation that those who have had three years in theological college can draw on. That is a serious danger, and can only be met by having regular in-service training for cell leaders, and by their readiness to refer difficult situations to the over-all pastor.

There is an undoubted danger in Christians being fascinated by the novel, and to many people cell church seems novel. Cells stand firmly in the renewal scene, which has proved so widespread and appealing in recent decades. But renewal that despises history and tradition can easily end up as neo-gnosticism. That is one danger that needs watching. Another is the mindless copying of one form of cell church that works, say, in Chile or Singapore without adapting it to one's own culture. Both Rob Merchant and Bob Hopkins give wise warnings about this. Once flexibility dies, so does the effectiveness of the cell.

I suppose one could add one further danger: the fragmentation of the congregation. That happens already, of course, when a church has different types of service early in the morning, midmorning and evening. These services draw different sectional congregations who may hardly ever meet, unless there are regular social occasions for all to join in. I think the same expedient is possible for cell churches. Occasional celebrations are a vital counterpoise to the small cells in which most of their Christian living is done.

Enough has been said to show that there are dangers in cell church, and no congregation or pastor should go in for it without careful thought, prayer, and the wholehearted backing of the church. But there are great advantages too, which you may feel outweigh the dangers.

Advantages of Cell Church

For all the dangers of cell church, it offers us so many advantages that it deserves to be confidently taken into the life of the mainline churches. We do not plead for cell to the exclusion of all else, but as a vigorous and proven way of deepening fellowship and facilitating evangelism.

Let us recall some of the advantages that have been well set out in the preceding pages by author after author. First, cell underlines the essential nature of church. Church is not somewhere we attend but something we are. This is fundamental. The church is all about people, and too often in the traditional church people have been subordinated to structures, buildings and overbearing clerical oversight. Church is the place down the road – rather than the believers in the street! All that changes with cell church. The pendulum swings firmly back to the biblical emphasis on the people of God. Nobody can mistake that when you meet in a home or army barracks, a hospital wing or a school – it banishes the heresy that the church is buildings.

Furthermore, cell reverses another heresy and shows that ministry is something the Lord expects of all his followers, not just the clergy and missionaries! Every-member ministry, a watchword of many a good church in the past 30 years, is never better demonstrated than in a cell church, where every member is obliged to contribute in discussion and giving, in service and outreach. When Wilson Carlisle, founder of the Church Army, was once asked why he played the trombone in the pulpit, he replied that it was to wake up the members of the congregation. Cell church does precisely that, and more effectively than any trombone.

Other advantages readily come to mind. In many circles, especially the pre-Christian or those so post-Christian that in effect they have never heard the gospel at all, the cell is by far the most attractive context into which to invite enquirers. The warmth, the laughter, the food, the involvement of one and all, the readiness to pray for one another and the determination to live out what they learn – all this is winsome. We must, however, pay attention to Bob Hopkins's caveat. In places where traces of Christendom remain, this emphasis on the dynamic, intentional cell can come as a threat and can smell like a cult. Equally in places where the concept of extended family remains strong, as in much of Africa and Samoa, the 'small wing' of the church is already in place, actually or potentially, and it would be folly to attempt to introduce cells into such a scene.

One of the most important advances made by the cell over the old home group is in the area of evangelism. The home groups, for the most part, did not engage in evangelism. They existed for the nurture and encourage-ment of the saints. But cell groups exist to multiply. In most countries they set a target of splitting in six months or at most a year. The assistant leader in the cell starts a new one with half the cell, and both groups set out to multiply again. This is a lesson we must energetically take on board in the West, where our evangelism is so weak. We may not do it precisely as they do in Singapore, but attractive cells are an invaluable way of breaking into our post-Christian culture. I shall never forget being asked by Albert Vun in Sabah to give an evangelistic address after a large dinner for over 400 people. 'But', he said, 'do not appeal for response. Everyone here is connected with a cell, and the friend that brought them will apply the message to their hearts.' Well, I was dubious. But how right he was. We ended the evening in his home, and it was marvellous to hear cell member after cell member calling him on the phone to say that they had been speaking to the friend they had welcomed to the dinner, and that friend had turned to Christ. That night I learnt the value of cells in evangelism. I doubt if there is any other method in use today, Alpha included, that is so effective.

Part of the joy of the cell is that it is magnificent at nurturing new believers. They are simply built up in the cell where they have been introduced to the faith. They already know and trust the leaders and the members. Why go to any extraneous nurture group? The cell is a brilliant and natural context both for evangelism and for subsequent nurture.

The cell has other advantages. It is highly flexible and is not bound by buildings. It does not even require a paid ministry. Moreover, as Mark Francisco has shown, cell lightens the senior pastor's pastoral load and allows him to concentrate on training the congregation. This is what he was trained for, but in a traditional church he so rarely has time to do it.

Cell is not the only effective way to restructure the church to serve postmodern society better. But it is certainly an important one, and I believe we shall hear a lot more of it. That is why my friends and I have got this book together. We believe cell is on the cutting edge of Christian advance in this century.

Cell, Church, Celebration and Community

Let me end this chapter by recording a visit my wife and I made to Canada this summer (2001). I believe it may be 'a cloud the size of a man's hand', pointing to a viable path for the future. We were invited by Southside Community Church, adjoining Vancouver. This unusual church had four worship centres, which it staffed with a central leadership team and worship team. Every Sunday the preacher and the musicians officiated at two venues. They possessed two church buildings and hired a cinema and a school. The two churches were packed, and there was a sizeable congregation in both cinema and school. It was deliberately informal, to make it natural for people in shorts and sandals to come in off the street, and this is just what they did. There was no liturgy: the menu was worship songs led by the band, a little prayer, the creed (curiously!) frequent adult baptisms, and an extensive sermon. Most of the people in all four congregations were converts who had little or no previous contact with the Christian faith.

All this was fine, but it certainly was not the heart of Southside. The heart of the church lay in the cells. You simply were not allowed to join the church until you joined a cell, where the main business of discipleship, sacrificial giving, ministry of various types and evangelism went on. The cells came together on a Sunday to worship the Lord in a relaxed setting that could appeal to the community: they called it 'church'. Casual churchgoers and visitors were invited to Alpha, which proved their main evangelistic tool. It worked well. So they had lots of converts, but in contrast to the pattern outlined in most of this book, the cells themselves were not designed for evangelism but for nurture and discipleship. Cell membership was tight, and the leaders were carefully trained both through a substantial manual and regular well-run corporate meetings.

Celebrations were held monthly, and the four congregations came together to celebrate the Lord with lively praise, good teaching and the Eucharist. This mobilised and unified the whole church for its outreach to the community.

What of the community at large? The churches impacted it in various ways. They showed new films (free) to all comers once a month. They ran a variety of sports camps for unchurched youngsters. They put on a superbly planned carnival in a park near each of the four worship centres, with free food and drink and the opportunity to sit in the sun and chat with the many visitors from the neighbourhood. But best of all was the Big Pig Gig which took place every Labour day. All the members of the church got involved. They put on a massive carnival in the street adjoining one of their worship locations, in a poor downtown area. They roasted three enormous pigs whole on spits overnight in the street, and invited everyone to come and freely enjoy. They did – some 3,000! There were inventive entertainments for all ages, a band, drama, a speaker and seating provided by an appreciative town council. Meanwhile church members wandered around chatting, and that afternoon around 200 people signed up for the next Alpha course. The whole thing was a delightful embodiment of the free grace of God, and a great day out for the family. The locals do not all stream into church after the Pig Gig, though some do: but they know where to go when they are in trouble. Through this community work the church has won an enviable reputation with the town council, the social workers and the local residents, and is having a significant impact on the area. Have they not hit on a brilliant combination? Cell, church, celebration, community. That is the balanced Christian life.

But in much of our Western Christianity we have lost three of those four elements. We have lost the joyful celebrations. We have lost the community events. And we have lost the cell. This book is written in the conviction that we need to recover all three. But it all begins with the radical values of the cell, and the determination to travel that route. When that is in place, the church will be invigorated, celebration will become a way of life, and a passion to impact the community with a flavour of Christ will result. Yes, it all begins with the cell.